A Tree,

A Reader on Arboreal Kinship

ONOMATOPEE 258

PHOTOSYNTHESIS
BY JORGE MENNA BARRETO

SIT STILL
AND READEFINE TIME
PLANT BOOKS
IN REVERSE
AND TREES WILL GROW
UNDER THE LIGHT

VEGETATE

UNDER THE SAME LIGHT
PAGES WILL GROW
IN VERSES
AS YOU FIND TIME
IN PLANT-PACED
LIFE

Introduction 4
Marjolein van der Loo

Anthropocene 15
Therolinguistics
Amirio Freeman

Trees with Added Color 18
Femke Habets

Untitled 21
Renée Bus

The Living Room 22
Roderick Hietbrink

From East Helsinki 26
Lockdown Diaries
Lucy Davis

Sentimentally Fierce 36
Mari Keski-Korsu

An Ovarian 40
Woolgathering
Manjot Kaur

How to Love a Tree, 42
Chapter III
Hira Nabi

The Sleep of Plants 44
Anne Richter

Birth Tree Ritual 58
Jonmar van Vlijmen

Who are you? (Vilka är ni?) 62
Ingela Ihrman

Silver Maple 64
Heemraadssingel
Alice Ladenburg

Luis' Oak Tree 66
Bárbara Sánchez Barroso

A Day in the Life of a Tree 70
Interspecies Library
(Oscar Salguero)

Trails of a Tree 80
Sanne Vaassen

Everything Goes in 83
Nature: Learnings from
the Plant Kingdom
Celine Baumann

Acorn / An Oak Tree / 91
Octavia E.
Müge Yilmaz

Ancestral Linden 94
Lemonade
Marjolein van der Loo

The Fox and the Linden 98
Frank Resseler

On a Trajectory Through 108
a Maze of Trajectories
Gerbrand Burger

20-07-2018 111
Jerrold Saija

Correction 115
Chihiro Geuzenbroek

Primordial Tongues or 117
the Language of
Non-Autonomous Beings
Karen Lofgren

Colonsay 120
Joss Allen

A Tree,

A Reader on Arboreal Kinship

A Tree, is the first iteration of a five-year program titled *A Tree, with a Bird, by a Woman, on Land, Under a Star,* which aims to build space for rich encounters between folklore and critical research. Beginning with *A Tree,* the project title grows each year with the addition of each subsequent chapter, and it also builds and changes in meaning as the actors and points of focus shift. The title becomes a phrase that functions as a kind of spell, made of exit points or components that comprise their own ecology of stories and characters. Together, they form a composition, like a tarot card reading that speaks to the future and the past, that shares an insight, a warning, or a recipe for the now. Through a multitude of forms, the project commissioned by Onomatopee activates its multipurpose project space, morphing the outcomes and exchanges between exhibition, public program, publication, and workshop with a myriad of actors.

A Tree, our beginning, is a research project about vegetal agency, plant knowledge, and the interaction between plants and people, with a specific focus on trees. Like all plants, trees make the world; they literally create soil, shape landscapes, and regulate the climate to some extent. They produce oxygen. They provide fuel, food, building materials, and shelter, and form ecologies where all kinds of species come together to enter into a myriad of symbiotic partnerships. Trees are wonderful to think with, and humans have been doing so—in all kinds of storytelling, through meditation, and as partners in problem-solving—probably for as long as they have walked the earth. Trees have been acknowledged as beings in relation; some trees are said to hold human spirits or form part-human hybrids, whether as punishment, blessing, or by choice.[1] In many Indigenous cultures, trees become humans, and humans become trees, bringing forth a kin-centric worldview in which trees and humans are considered equals; relatives.[2]

Trees such as linden and oak have been central to ceremonies and witnesses of rituals in many European countries. They hold meaning, power, and stories. Territorially, many trees are used as monuments and signifiers, often of borders, and as borders. Trees that produce nutmeg, rubber, and timber have been central to colonial extractivism. The power that trees hold can be both life-giving and destructive, sometimes facilitated by human mismanagement.

Trees specifically can teach us much about planetary survival. They have lived on the Earth for up to 420 million years and have thrived through multiple disasters and existentially impactful changes. Trees are the embodiment of the seasons and indicators of climate changes and the current emergency. The older a tree, the more experience it has and the more (climate) resilient its descendants will be. That is one of many reasons why old trees are extremely important. Some tree species,

1   The interpretation of, and reason for the transformation varies: the becoming of a tree can be experienced as a punishment and portrayal of character like in Lithuanian folk story Eglė the Queen of Serpents. But the transformation can also be a form of reward and escape from danger, as in the Greek story of Baucis and Philemon, Daphne, and that of Myrrha.

2   Catriona A. H. Sandilands, 'Timber. Douglas-fir. Art', in Laura Drouet & Olivier Lacrouts (eds.), *Plant Fever* (Boussu: Stichting Kunstboek, CID au Grand-Hornu, 2020).

such as pines and Japanese cypress trees, can live up to between 5,000 and 10,000 years. They stretch their lives over periods of time we humans can hardly imagine. The climate disruption crisis we face partly stems from people's inability or unwillingness to think and plan far ahead. Trees are also time tellers. Forester Peter Wohlleben says people often misunderstand trees, mainly because they are so slow. We can apply the concept of tree time here; rather than following industrial time, clock time, or any time defined by human activity, trees relate to their own experience of time.

Another element of the climate problem stems from modern individualism, which has weakened, if not erased, our relationships with earlier ancestors and future generations. On this front, trees also have much to teach us about community and how to be there for each other. Forest ecologists like Suzanne Simard and the anthropologist Anna Tsing have written much about the interaction between trees, the complex ecological structures of forests, and the significant collaboration with fungi. According to Simard, a forest is a socialist community in which resources pass between trees via mycorrhizal networks. The exchange of sugars and minerals not only exists for subsistence but can also be an exchange of distress signals to warn about predators and threats.[3]

Thanks to tree time and tree community, trees can be particularly valuable companions when thinking outside of our human lifespans and provide inspiration and encouragement to consider complex ecologies. They call

3   Read more in Suzanne Simard, *Finding the Mother Tree* (London: Penguin Books, 2022); and Anna Tsing, *Mushroom at the End of the World* (Princeton: Princeton University Press, 2015).

us to collaborate with and learn from vegetal life, to recognize its abilities and agency. However, there can be pitfalls to this approach, too. Trees should be acknowledged as intelligent and communicative in a careful manner; their nature as a vastly different species should be respected. It would be restrictive and reductive to see trees as slow and old humans. To what extent, then, can anthropomorphism strengthen the connection between humans and trees, and when does it become an anthropocentric danger that makes it impossible to learn from such rich vegetal knowledge?

The project *A Tree*, admires the magnificent existence of forests, taking trees sometimes as a species and sometimes as individual actors as it aims to invoke a close relationship with and reflect on trees as both beings and keepers of wisdom. Nonetheless, it's impossible to isolate a tree, the holobiont that houses, feeds, and provides for hundreds of species.[4] We identify with trees as individuals and see somewhat of a mirror image of ourselves. Similarly, we forget that we are – as Amirio Freeman beautifully paraphrases Astrida Neimanis in *Plantcraft* – "[...] holobionts — multi-entity soups — with our guts full of microorganisms, our bodies fecund with water, and our ancestry shared with the entire expanse of life on Earth—including plants. Our lives being weaved together by the living and by the dead."[5] Like trees, each human is always and already a multispecies community.

4   A holobiont is an assembly of a host and the numerous other species that coexist with it and who, together, create an ecological system through symbiosis.

5   Amirio Freeman, "PLANTCRAFT: Oscar Salguero Finds Possibility in Fictional Plants," PLANTCRAFT, April 16, 2024, https://plantcraft. substack.com/p/plantcraft-oscar-salguero-finds-possibility.

Many trees hold the physical and visual memories of crafts, communication, and extraction. Barks and trunks can function as books that hold ideas and visualize practices that date back centuries, both human and more-than-human. Like many foresters, this publication uses a bright color to communicate observations, information, requests, or plans on and about trees. Despite this book being printed on wood-free paper, for centuries, tree-based cellulose has been the primary medium for the gathering and reproducing of ideas. Siddhartha Gautama attained enlightenment and became Buddha under the Banyan or Bodhi tree. In a similar vein, Yggdrasil, the sacred tree in the Norse and Germanic pagan mythologies, offers Odin eternal knowledge after a sacrifice by hanging himself from a branch. Eternal knowledge refers to the technology of writing, the system of runes, storing wisdom without the risk of fading or forgetting. The physicality of the tree, later contributing to the production of paper, can then be seen to play a role in that storage, too, as a safe of information.

The exhibition *A Tree*, taking place from mid-July to mid-September in the summer of 2024, is the first expression of *A Tree, with a Bird, by a Woman, on Land, Under a Star*. It brings together a variety of perspectives and projects that each have their own mix of criticality, craft, labor, poetry, technology, humor, and thorough research. It showcases research and works where artists explore and address the relationship between people and trees and ways in which we can relate more closely to their time span.

The video work *Living Room* by Roderick Hietbrink depicts an event involving an oak tree and a furnished living room through which the tree is dragged. Humoristic, absurd, shocking, and confusing, the short film shows a simple but violent event that puts human-tree relations on display and raises questions of victim and perpetrator. In this publication, Roderick shares behind-the-scenes documentation revealing how humans set up the oak in the video.

Manjot Kaur produces speculative fiction by mixing ancient mythologies with fantasy to question the relationship between people and more-than-humans, creating possibilities for a post-queer and post-human world. Her work *Portrait of a Tree in a Jharokha III*, meticulously painted with bright and colorful gouache on wasli paper, depicts a tree as a ruler or acknowledges them as always and already so. Within a fictional text, Manjot shares a piece of writing that entangles the world she paints with reality as a multi-sensory physical experience.

The work *How to Love a Tree III* by Hira Nabi is a selection of crayon rubbings on silk made in the blue pine forests of Murree and the Galiyat region of Pakistan. Hira sees these tourist destinations as crumbling ecosystems with a history marked by colonial rule. The print in this book is a cyanotype from the same forest. A snapshot and a representation of the location that carries the history of and relationships between people and trees linked to mutilation, communication, healing practices, and extraction.

Much of Gerbrand Burger's artistic practice comes from sustainable forestry and an interest in embedding art in natural processes. The artist's sculpture *Models for Deep Storage* is made from sustainably sourced birch wood and presents five miniatures for future sculptures on a tabletop. Each object shows characteristics of repository use, while its shapes refer to modernist icons and Bauhaus style. With the ideas of modernity encapsulated in each sculpture, they are returned to their original habitat and slowly digested within their ecosystem. In the publication, Gerbrand shares how a life-size sculpture is installed within its intended habitat of the forest.

The video *Trees of Rotterdam* by Alice Ladenburg and Ollie Palmer investigates the relationship between trees and public space and their role in urban planning. The film's black background contrasts with the sharp white point-cloud images made using high-tech scanners. It situates the relationship between people and trees using the age of trees to illustrate layers of time that outlive buildings and people in the city. In this publication, Alice shares her observations of a maple tree that was part of her research on urban trees in Rotterdam.

From personal observations of a tree in the urban space in front of her house, Sanne Vaassen developed the work *Fractals*, an installation consisting of ten metal towers and four slide projectors. The towers house every leaf that the artist gathered from one elm tree during one fall season. A collection of about twelve thousand leaves is archived in transparent folders, and a selection of photo frames is beamed onto the walls. The elaborate, laborious, and once-in-a-lifetime project for the artist adds complexity to the seemingly self-evident and cyclical event enacted by the tree. In the book, Sanne shares the notations of where she found each leaf, revealing yet more of the meticulous collection process.

We also find the work *Spruce Time* by Goldin+Senneby in the exhibition, two photo prints of the oldest spruce tree in the world, approximately 9550 years of age. The prints document part of the long-term collaboration project with a hospital in Malmö, Sweden, in which the artist duo attempted to clone the tree through grafting.

Finally, a successful clone will be planted in its own care facility and share the climate with the clinic as a living memory of another time.

The video *The Wandering Spruce* by Ingela Ihrman zooms into the micro-history of spruce trees in the Nordic countries. In a scaled costume, the artist reenacts a cone dispersing seeds on Finland's coastline. With lightness and humor, the survival of a species and foundations for international human relations built through forest industries are sowed. In this publication, you can find sketches of multiple actors in a theater performance in which the character of the Wandering Spruce is featured.

As part of the *A Tree*, project, this publication can be seen as a continuation of the exhibition. It makes space for aspects of the work and research of each artist that were challenging to include physically in the show, given our limited time and resources. Among those aspects are the possibility of diving into intimate experiences, the queering qualities of trees, multi-sensory engagement through consumption, and historical contexts of human-tree relations and depictions. Through this reader, the aim is to nurture and further these dialogues and to share inspiration on exercising arboreal kinship by taking the time to think about trees differently, through imagination, art, music, storytelling, poetry, and images. Moreover, the contributions inspire us to move beyond large systems of oppression and towards exorcizing anthropocentrism, capitalism, individualism, heteronormativity, and coloniality.

The book also includes contributions from an additional group of cultural practitioners whose practices strongly relate to trees. These are all people whose work I admire and, in some cases, whom I have had the chance to work with in the past. Additionally, the short story by the late Anne Richter, first read to me by my friend Emma Clear, has inspired me greatly and is therefore included. A selection of images and artworks from the National Archives of the Netherlands, the London-based Wellcome Collection, and the New York Metropolitan Museum of Art provide some historical and visual context. Please note that all three of these collections were founded from a colonial, white, and Christian perspective — a viewpoint that is at the root of how Western society (mis)-treats trees. However, the book aims to add a critical perspective, nurture a collaborative mindset, and contribute to a growing awareness of this history.

KNOTS AND NODES

The book's order of contributions is intuitively chosen, resulting in a wild, 'orderless' variety of ideas. Each segment is attributed to one or more tags that relate to its content. These markers share the perspective of the editor and highlight the thematics or concerns of each work in the context of the publication.

ANCESTRAL

refers to a strong connection and countability to human and/or more-than-human life that came before us; intergenerational.

COMMUNICATIVE

is used when the work reflects on (alternative) ways of exchanging information and interpretation.

COMMUNAL

is used when work invites collectivity, exchange, and social activity.

DECOLONIAL

is used when the work itself is made with a specific aim to promote decolonial processes of healing and/or to critique modernity/coloniality.

EMBODIED is understood as encapsulated (knowledge) within the body and/or focused on a physical, tangible, somatic experience within and about bodies.

FOLKLORIC relates to generational knowledges transferred through stories, nature religions, and ecocentric belief systems with a timeless spirit.

INTIMATE refers to a close familiarity with the physical, often experienced as private.

QUEER is used as weird, out of the ordinary, surreal, and not corresponding to conventional ideas. Sometimes but not always related to gender and sex.

SCIENTIFIC refers to scientific research, using scientific or academic methods or structures to gather and share knowledge.

SENSORY refers to the engagement of multiple senses.

SPECULATIVE refers to fiction, imagination, or a trope that consciously moves beyond facts to adopt a starting point not experienced yet.

SPIRITUAL refers to a focus on soul or spirit and an experience of a cosmic or divine interconnectedness or entity.

With the exception of two commissioned contributions, all content of the book has been shared without financial compensation. I invited thinkers and makers I admire to share material that represents their work and that speaks to the project. I am very grateful and in debt to all these wonderful people who have given their time, effort, and work in contributing to this book. Initially, I hoped a few people I contacted would say yes and would have something lying around that they might like to publish as self-promotion. Somehow, and unexpectedly, everyone I contacted was excited, generously sharing what has created an untamable muddle of trees. Quite fitting. I very proudly introduce you to:

Joss Allen, Céline Baumann, Bárbara Sánchez Barroso, Jorge Menna Barreto, Gerbrand Burger, Renée Bus, Lucy Davis, Amirio Freeman, Chihiro Geuzenbroek, Femke Habets, Roderick Hietbrink, Ingela Ihrman, Manjot Kaur, Mari Keski-Korsu, Alice Ladenburg, Karen Lofgren, Hira Nabi, Frank Resseler, Anne Richter, Jerrold Saija, Oscar Salguero, Sanne Vaassen, Jonmar van Vlijmen, Müge Yilmaz.

Marjolein van der Loo

ANTHROPOCENE THEROLINGUISTICS:
ON QUAKING ASPENS AND THE EMERGENCE
OF A NEW THEROLINGUISTIC MOVEMENT
BY AMIRIO FREEMAN

The following is a preview of an article in the forth-coming 2030 issue of the *Journal of the Association of Therolinguistics.*[1]

Catastrophic heatwaves, microplastics-saturated oceans — signs of the so-called Anthropocene, this unfolding epoch of anthropogenic forces destabilizing Earth's equilibrium in pursuit of extraction, growth, and profit, disfigure the planet.

In response to a rapidly shifting planetary reality, every organism on Earth is adapting how it communicates, prompting the emergence of a new movement in the field of therolinguistics that I refer to as *Anthropocene Therolinguistics.*

Anthropocene Therolinguistics aims to observe how nonhuman languages have evolved alongside climate disruption, provoking innovative communicative techniques and a new set of primary concerns and themes present across a broad swath of contemporary more-than-human translations.

1 "Therolinguistics" is a speculative field of study dedicated to the study of the languages of more-than-human entities imagined by science fiction writer Ursula K. LeGuin in her short story *The Author of the Acacia Seeds and Other Extracts from the Journal of the Association of Therolinguistics* featured in her short story collection *The Compass Rose.* Much gratitude to (real-life!) archivist, book curator, and independent researcher Oscar Salguero for navigating me to this ingenious work.

Amirio Freeman - Anthropocene Therolinguistics

The latest therolinguistic literature is rich with evidence of this movement. Mexico's Dr. Efraín Flores published a paper on water-dwelling species who communicate with kinetic strategies integrating human refuse—Diet Coke cans, abandoned headphones—into their linguistic practices.

In my studies, I have brought the attention of therolinguists to a change in the percussive choral music of quaking aspens (*Populus tremuloides*), a tree species found throughout North America.

Therolinguists have long recorded and deciphered the aspen's signature acoustics, produced by wind passing through the tree's heart-shaped leaves. As now well-known, specific features of the tree's hum include the repetitive use of *We*, demonstrating a deep-seated communalist ontology; an emphasis on an ever-present *Now*; and an appreciation for life above- and belowground.

With AI-assisted photo analysis technology, my lab has tracked a gradual, near-imperceptible change in the aspen's leaf structure, creating a never-before-recorded variant of the tree's singular sound. The resulting tune suggests growing anxiety among the trees over an increasingly inhospitable biosphere; below is the first-ever published excerpt of this new iteration.

Here, We are Each Other's sowing
Here, We are Each Other's reaping

In the Dark, We are long
In the Below, We assemble Myself

Here, We are Each Other's sowing
Here, We are Each Other's reaping

In the Light, We are short
In the Above, We assemble
[a previously undocumented quaking aspen
sound that loosely translates to "nothing"]

Here, We are Each Other's sowing
Here, We are Each Other's reaping

(FROM THE COLLECTION)
TREES WITH ADDED COLOR
BY FEMKE HABETS

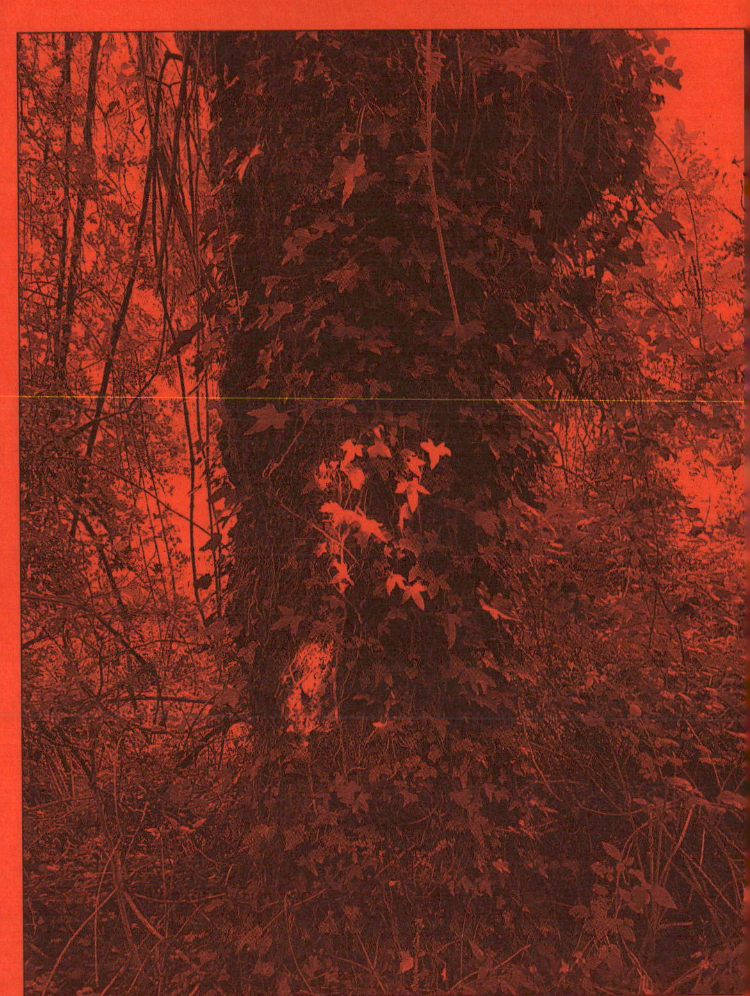

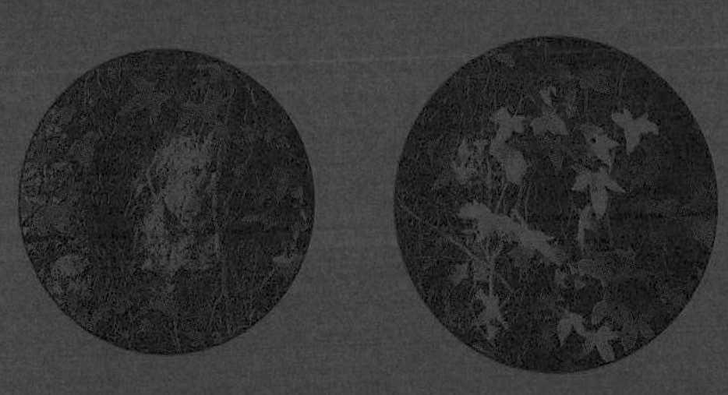

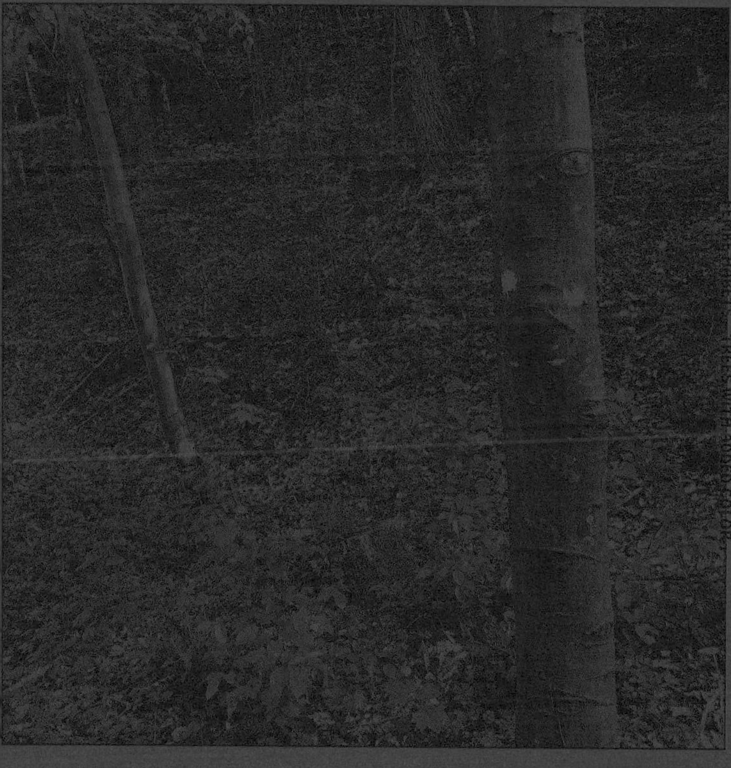

FEMKE HAREN? — TREES WITH ADDED COLOR

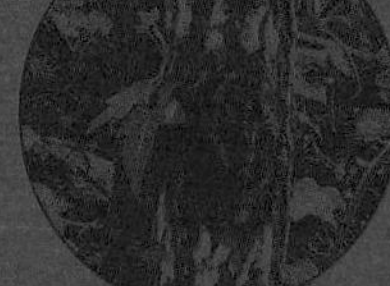

2019-NLMAA-001904F

Untitled
by Renée Bus

Walking alone,
letting footsteps be unheard.

Looking up,
at the crown of trees,
a saturated green,
it unfurls slowly after winter.

What begins with a growing mist,
after a few weeks has flowered
countless new leaves.

If a Beech has had a
chance to grow free,
its branches touching the earth.

Under the canopy of its
boughs when one sings.

Not only is it a
tangible cathedral but also
one that like it,
rings.

PHOTO REGISTRATION OF THE FILM SHOOT OF "THE LIVING ROOM", 2010

BY RODERICK HIETBRINK
PHOTOGRAPHY: JOS WESDIJK

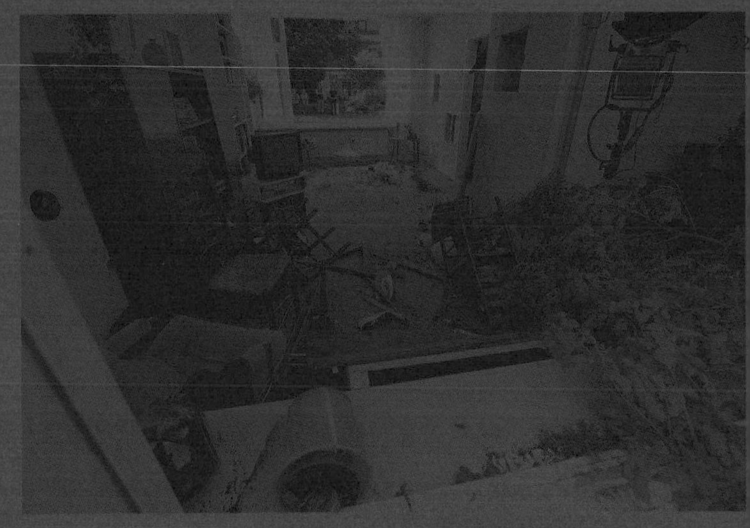

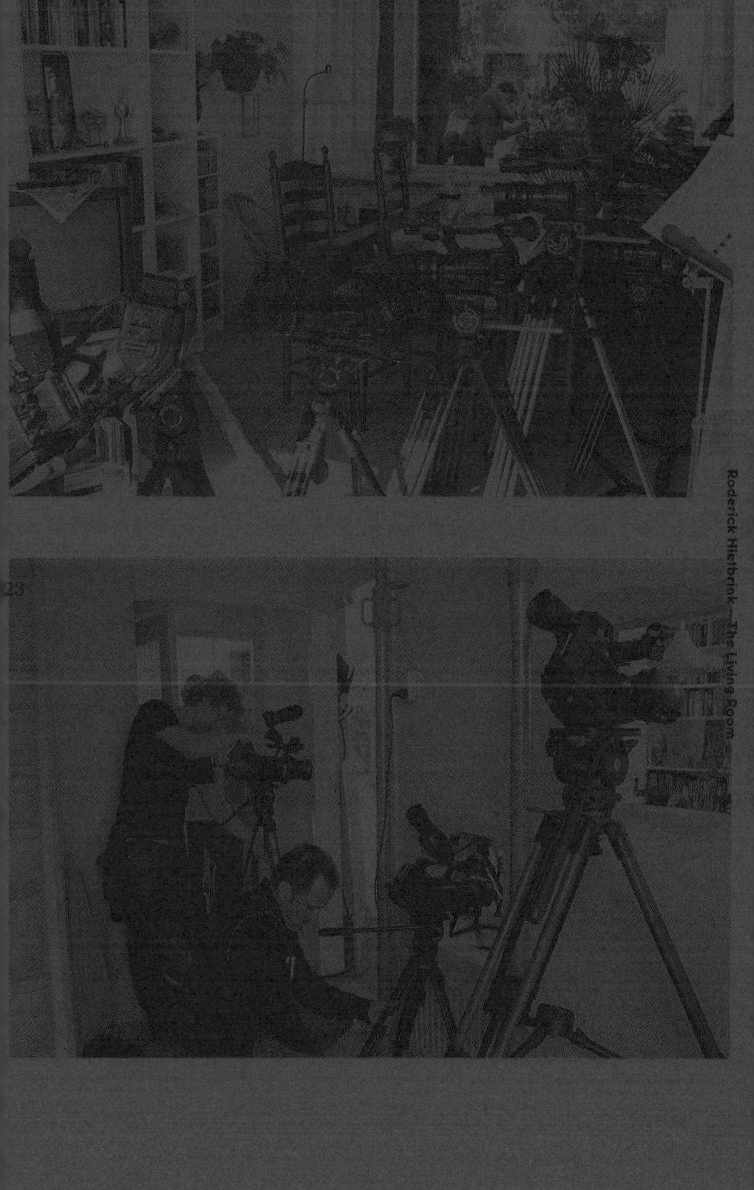

Roderick Hietbrink — The Living Room

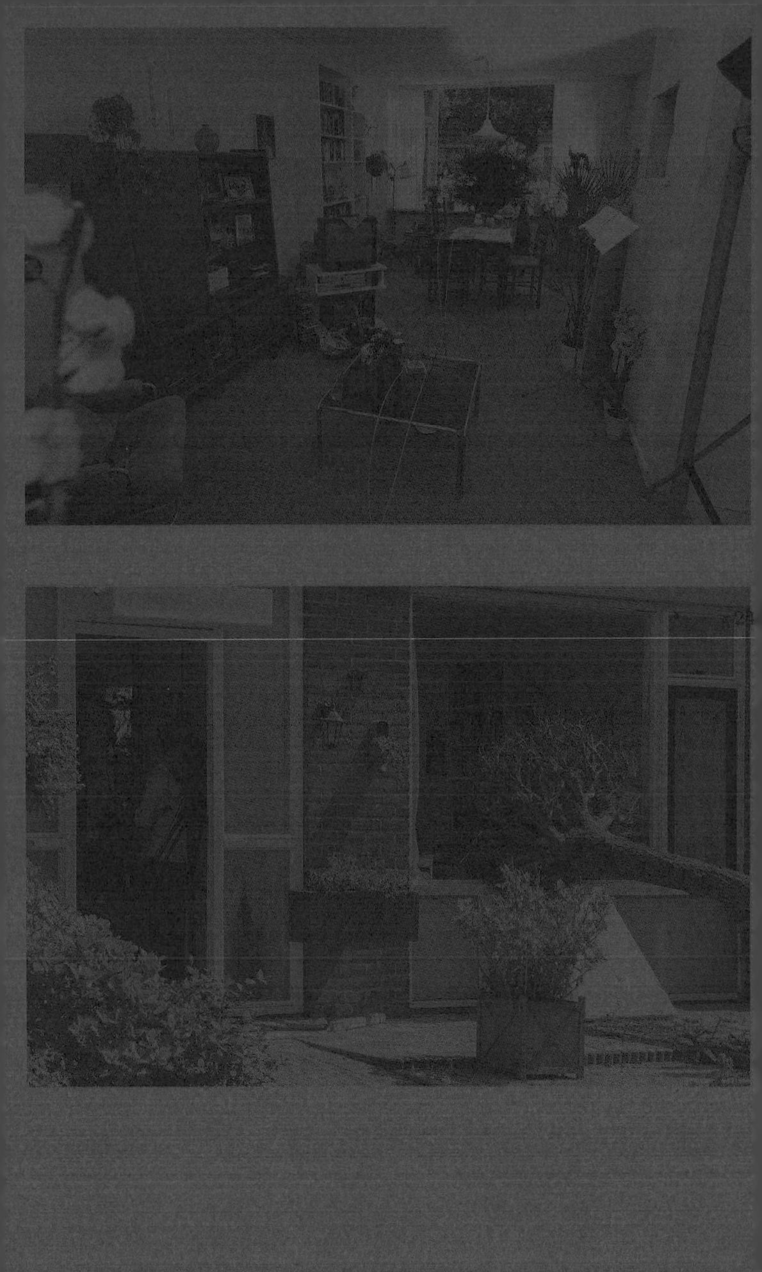

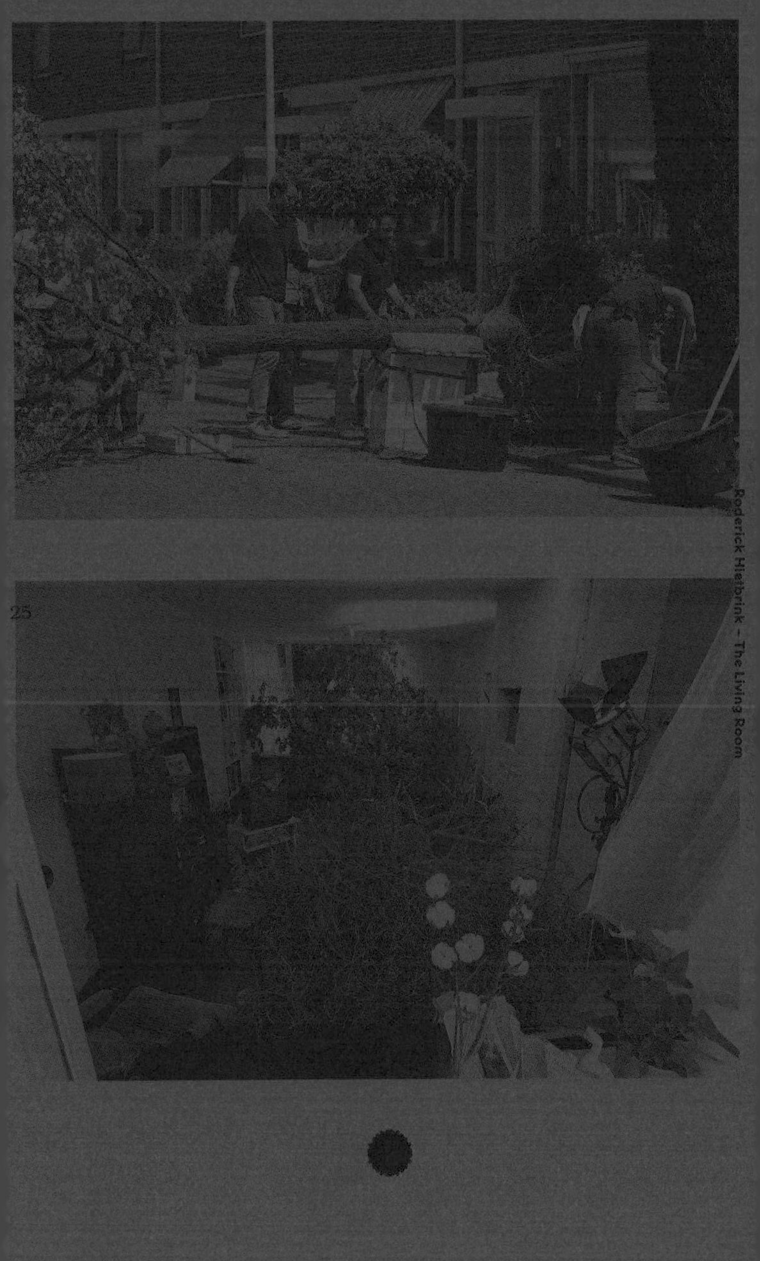
Roderick Hietbrink – The Living Room

From East Helsinki Lockdown Diaries
by Lucy Davis

There is a ball shaped, crack-willow in front
of my flat by the sea in East Helsinki, that
seems to constantly be asking people to sit with
it, or stand beside it, with their dogs, or their
bicycles, and look out towards the horizon.

The sea was like a mirror one early April
morning although some ice had formed in the
night over towards Kallahti bay. The red-
bonnet, winter-bather, granny club were out
there, chirpy as usual at 7am, speaking softly
to each other so as not to wake the neighbours,
and scooping away the soft ice-porridge that
had congealed around the steps with their
gloved hands as they entered the water to swim.

And then a little later another woman came
walking over from our block. She bathes alone
and always a little after the others, always
dressed in the same long, hooded, midnight-
blue house-cape, and always carrying a basket
for her towel and wet swimsuit.

The wind had picked up as she toweled herself
dry and dressed after her swim, framed in
silhouette as she was by the still leafless willow.
And then, for one brief moment, a cloud of
chattering sparrows rose up from the tree, and
off in all directions, as the small waves caught
the sunlight, and she drew her hood back over
her silver hair.

Lucy Davis – From East Helsinki Lockdown Diaries

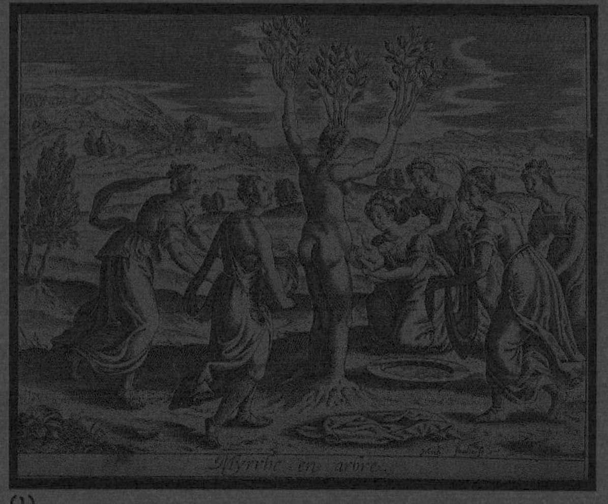

(1)

(2)

(3)

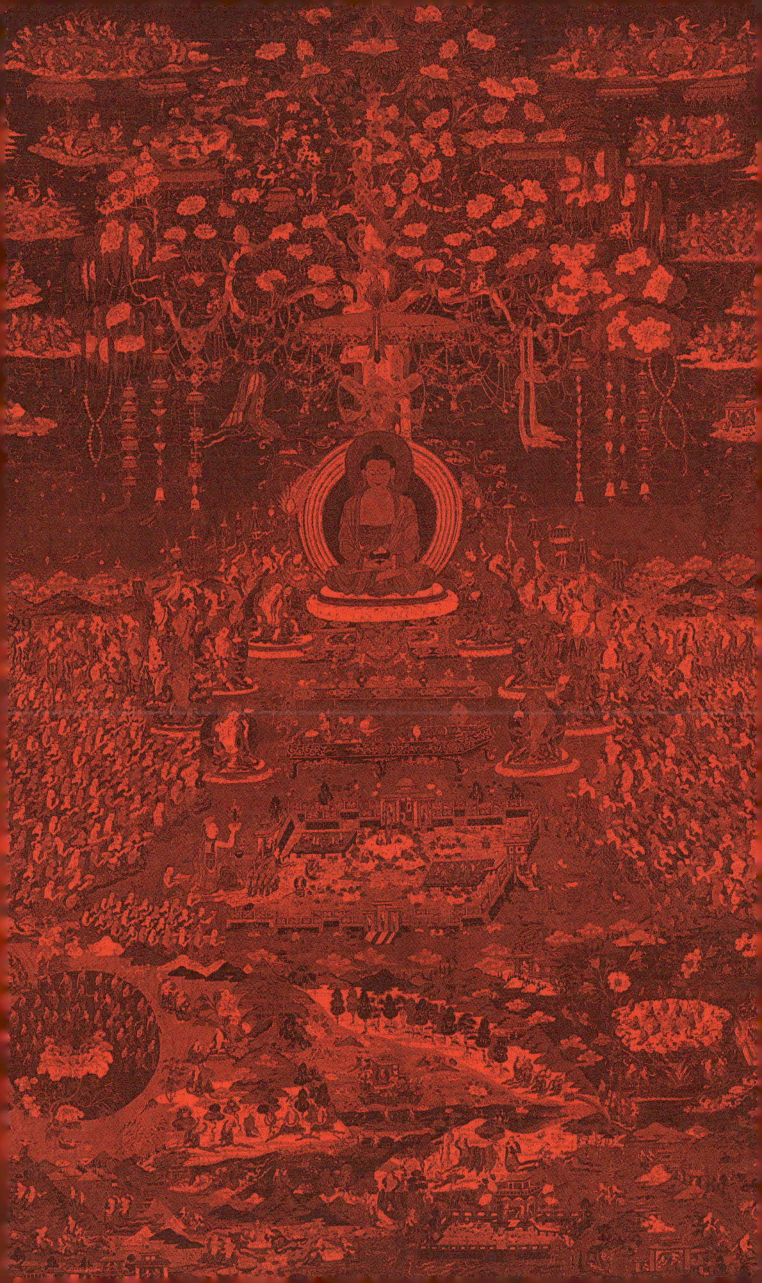

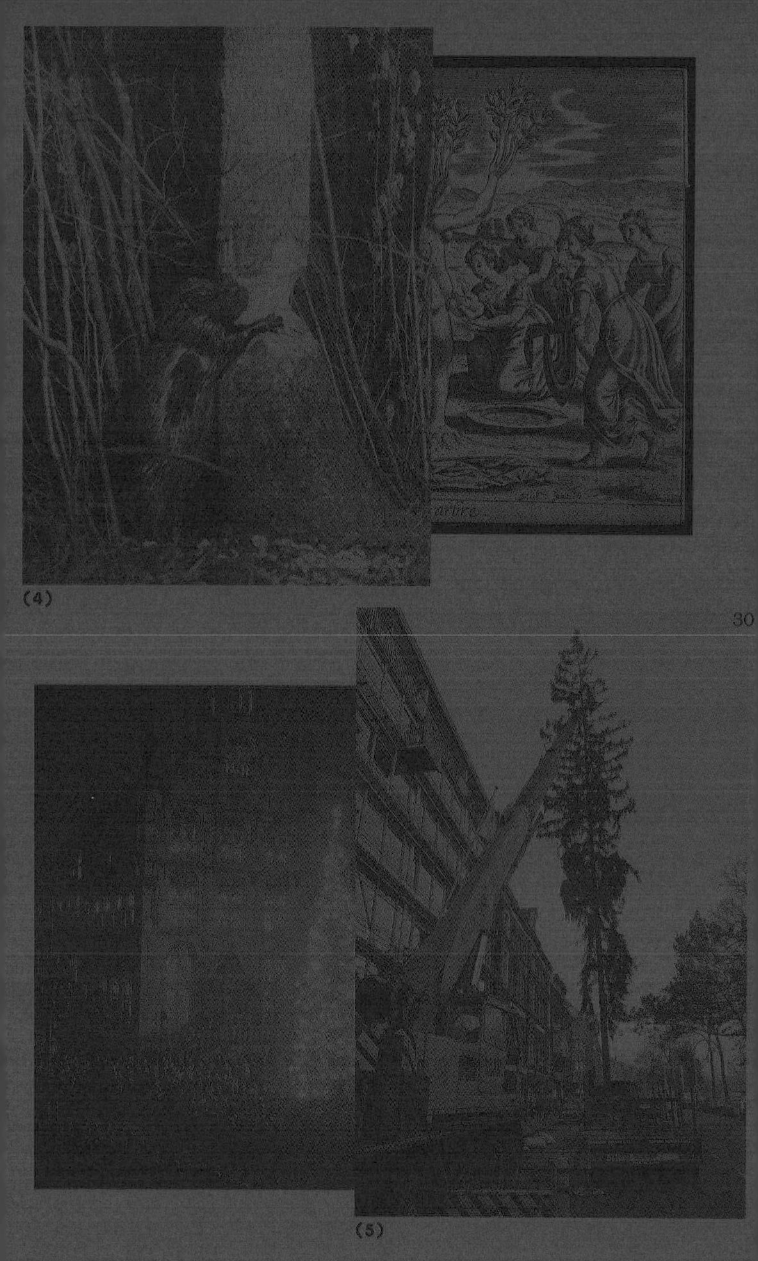

(4)

(5)

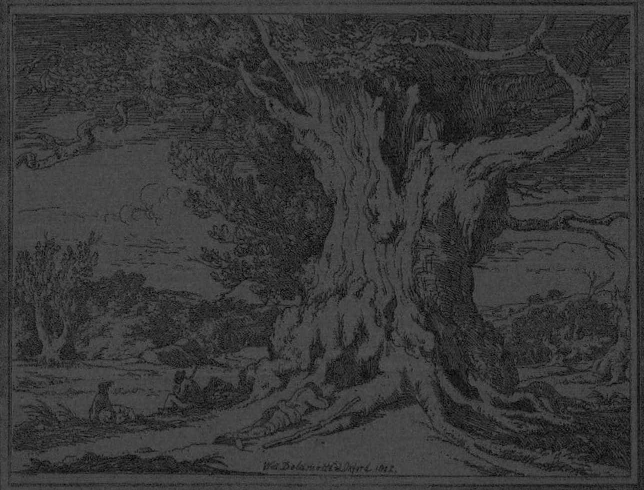

(6) 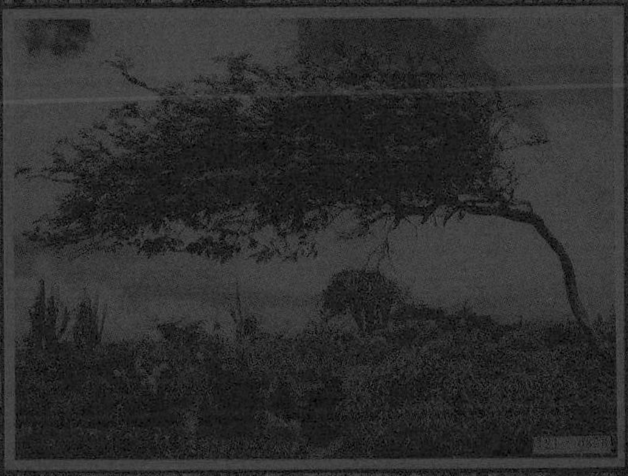
Wm Delamotte del. Oxford. 1808.
(7)

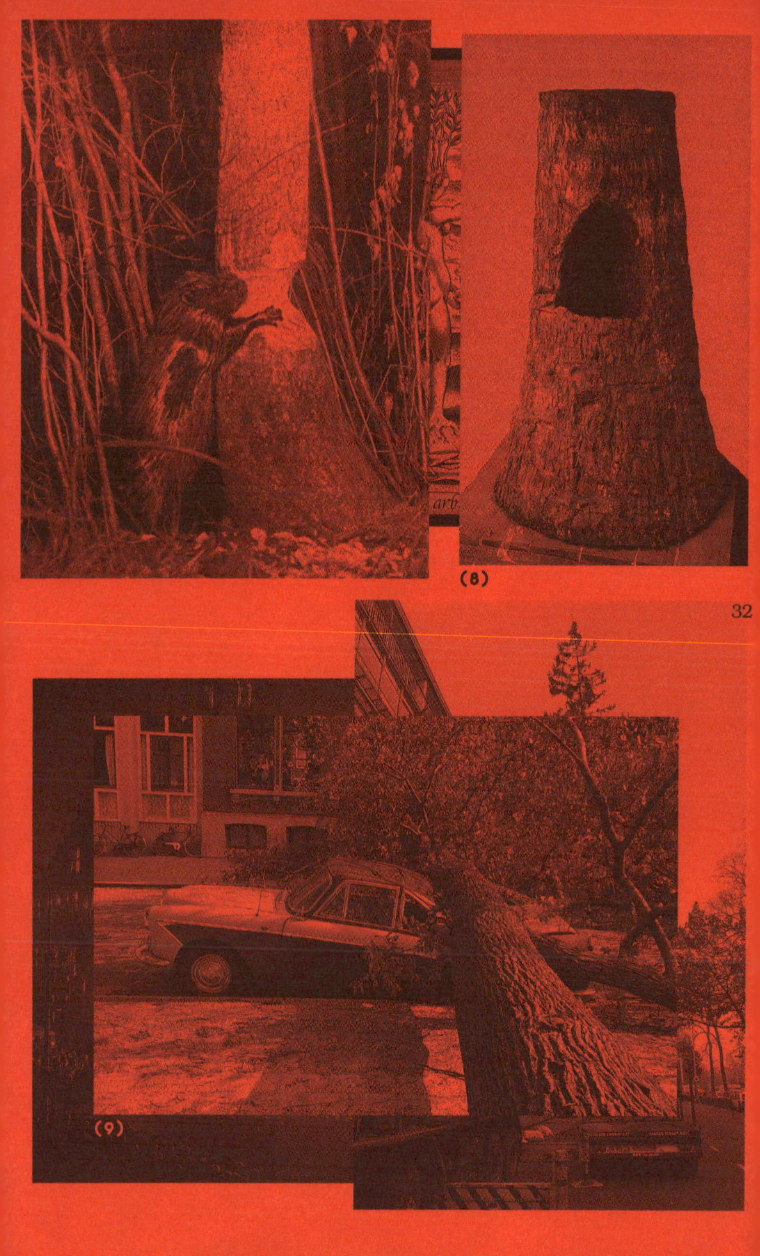
(8)
(9)

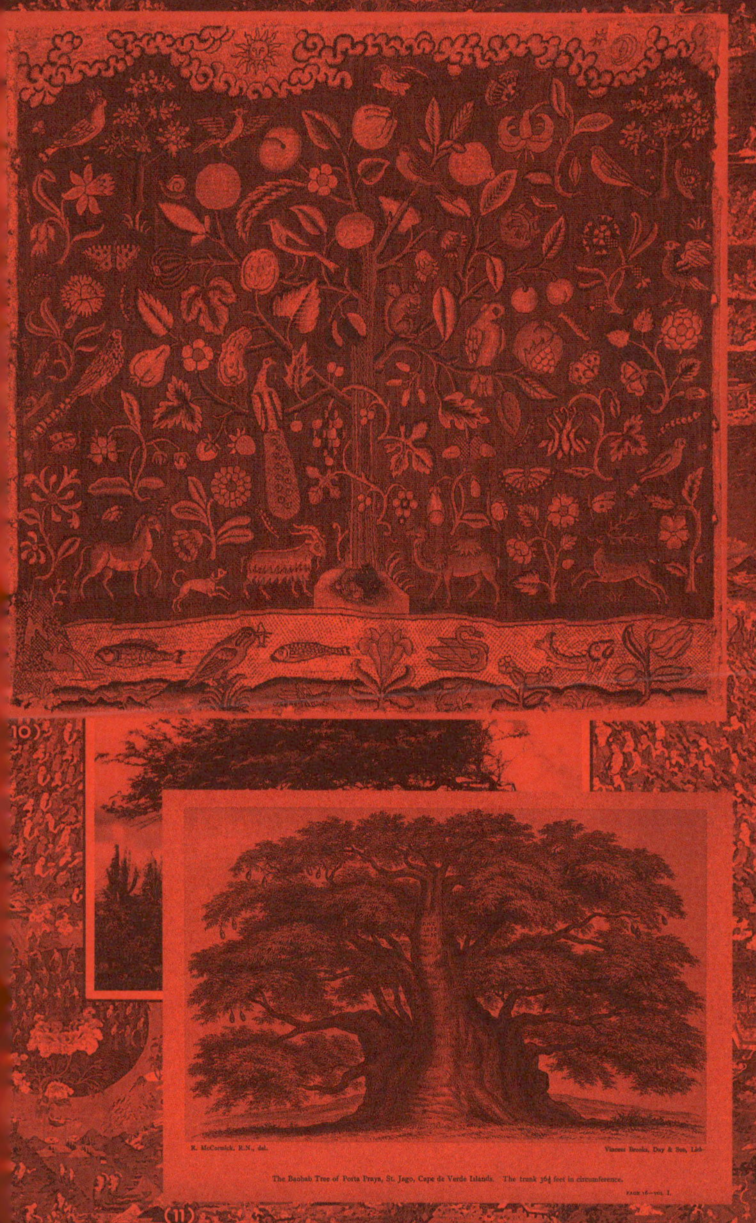

R. McCormick, R.N., del.

Vincent Brooks, Day & Son, Lith.

The Baobab Tree of Porta Praya, St. Jago, Cape de Verde Islands.   The trunk 36½ feet in circumference.

PAGE 16—VOL. I.

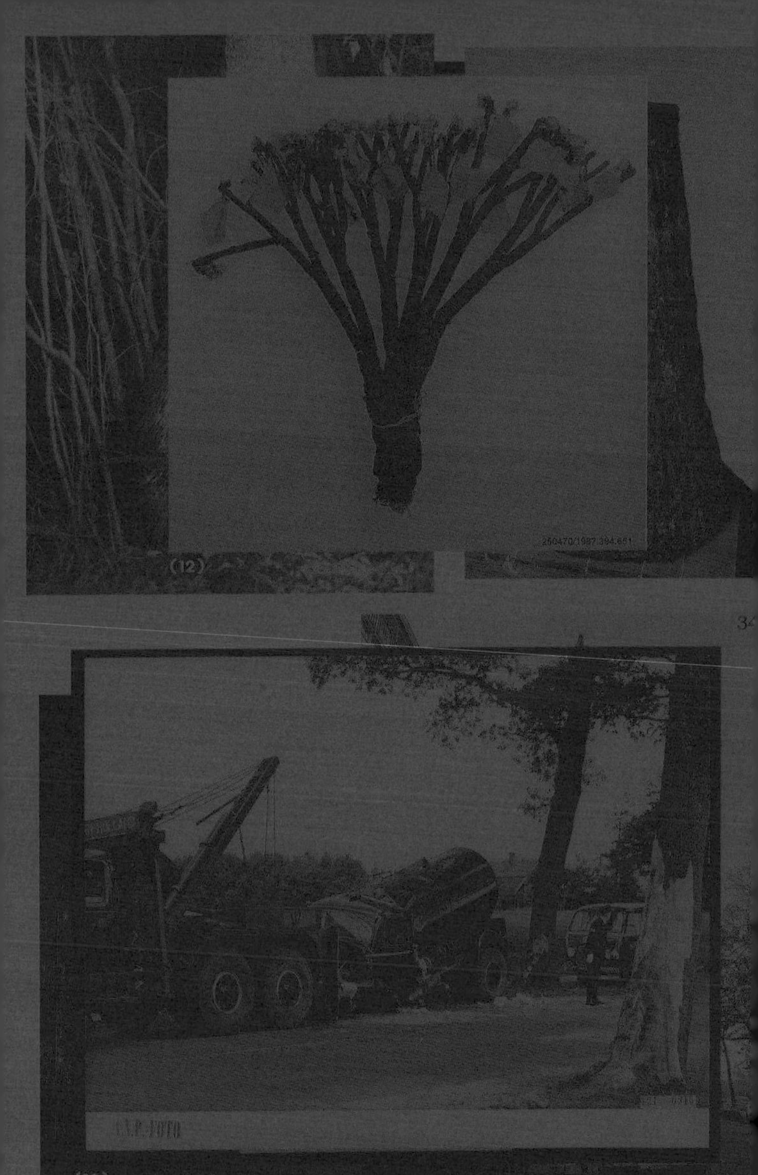
(12)
250470/1987.394.651
G.V.P. FOTO
(13)

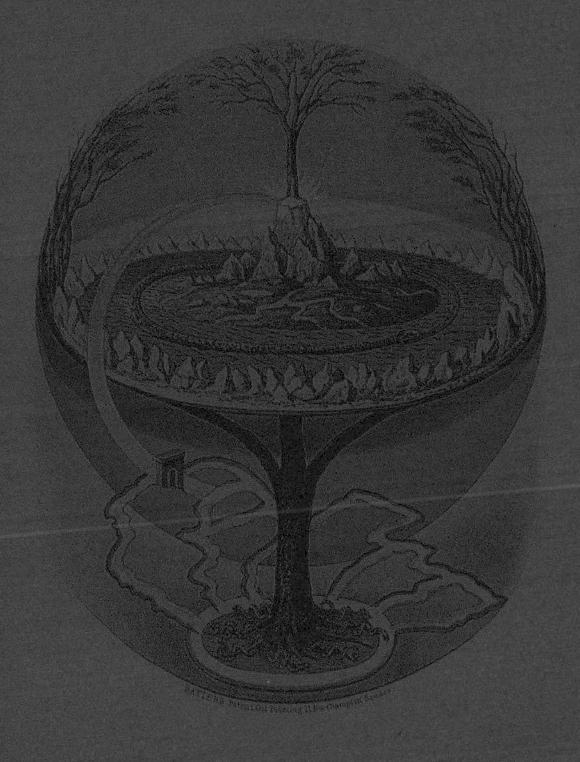

YGGDRASILL,

The Baobab Tree of Porto Praya, St. Jago, Cape de Verde Islands. The trunk 36 feet in circumference.

ANCESTRAL   COMMUNICATIVE   COMMUNAL   DECOLONIAL
EMBODIED   FOLKLORIC   INTIMATE   QUEER
SCIENTIFIC   SENSORY   SPECULATIVE   SPIRITUAL

Participatory Performance
SENTIMENTALLY FIERCE
by Mari Keski-Korsu and Birch, 2024

As part of Feral Fields: Practicing with More-than-Human
Vartiosaari, Helsinki, Finland.

"Last summer, I had a very intense
encounter with this birch tree that fell
down in Vartiosaari (Island in east
Helsinki). I simply could not pass by them.
I thought I should witness, grief and
meditate with the transformation, but
there was like a slap on my face saying:
don't be so sentimental! Thus, I climbed
up to the trunk and walked barefoot all
the way to the top. It felt like walking
vertically to the sky, my soles were full
of joy, all the formations, the scents of
leaves, and composting matters. Inspired
by this, I attempted to facilitate a new
encounter this summer. It was a celebration
of an elder: combining barefoot walking,
plant medicine, and folklore related to
birch (namely runosongs acknowledging
more-than-human ancestors)."

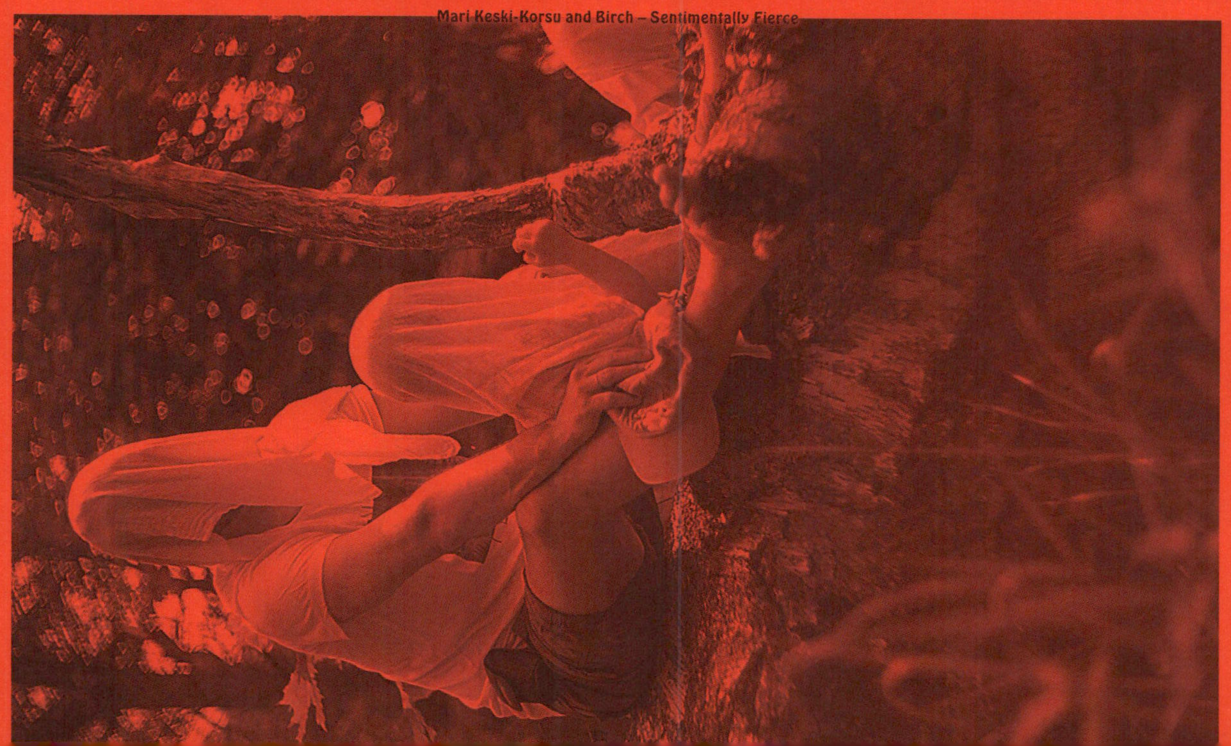

Mari Keski-Korsu and Birch – Sentimentally Fierce

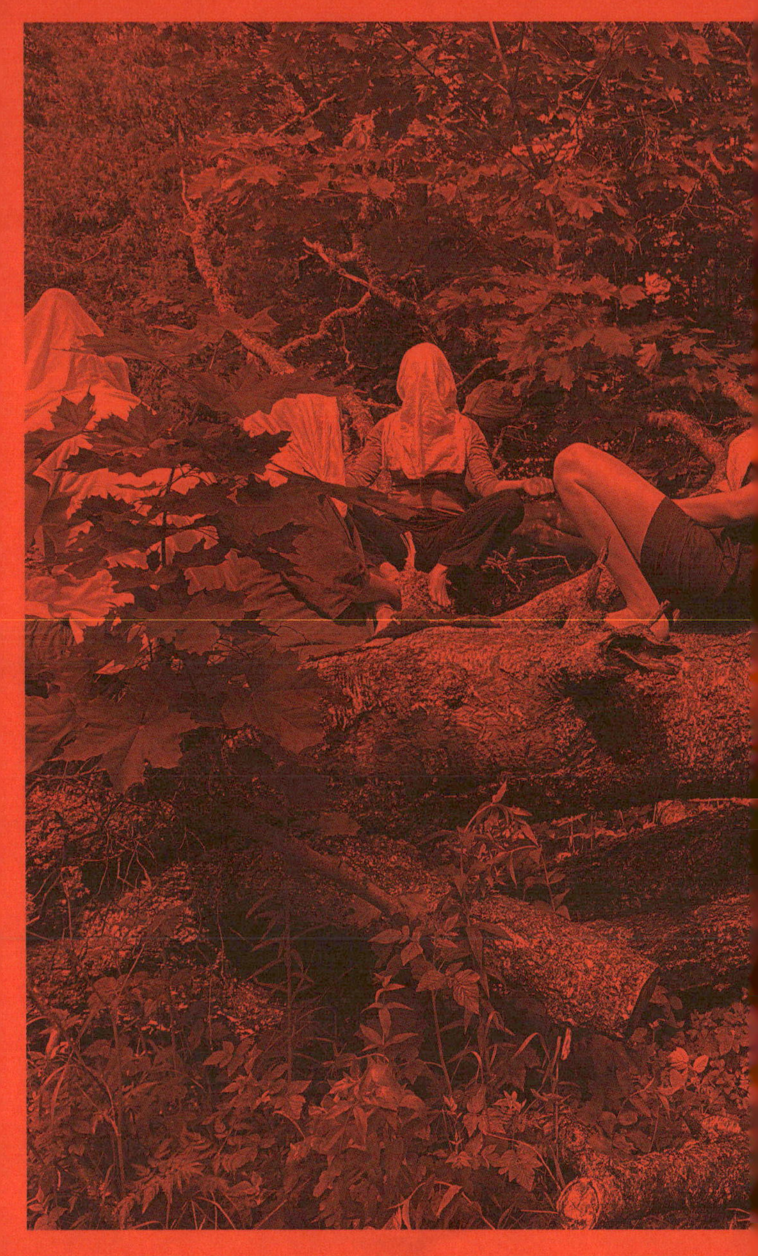

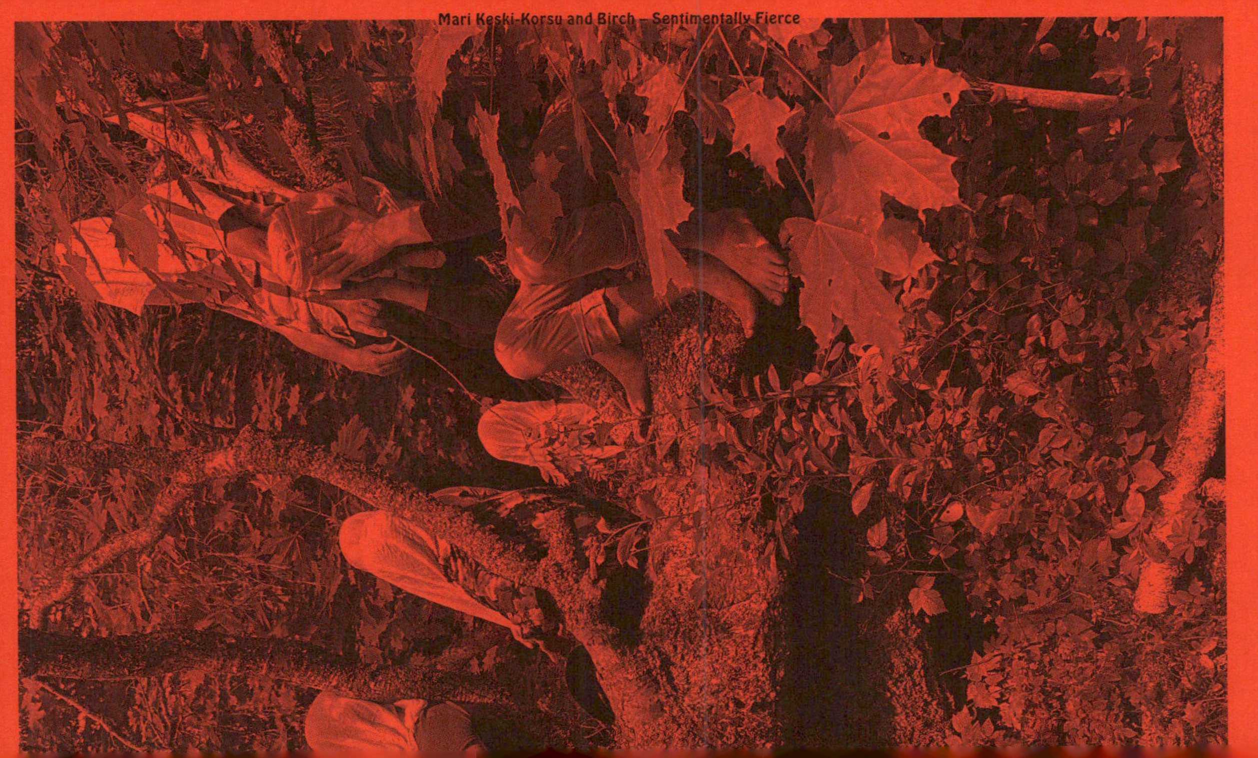

Mari Keski-Korsu and Birch – Sentimentally Fierce

AN OVARIAN WOOLGATHERING
BY MANJOT KAUR

The other day, I was observing hair on my legs and wondered if I should wax them today or later on the weekend. My lazy self is always procrastinating the process and enjoys wandering in the micro-world of porous skin and hair. As I observed, my sight fell on a cluster of hair on my vulva, and I noticed a new strange growth. The hair seemed to be metamorphosing into emerald-green grass and feathery moss. A high-pitched scent of the grass and a fermented fragrance entered my nostrils. There was a new texture to the air, a moistness.

My body started to adjust to its weather, deep time, and ecology. I did not know that sneaking into this pocket of moss growing on my body was to directly step into this vibrant zone of profound interconnectedness and intertwined semiotic systems. This, in turn, untangled my senses and the rhythm of my breath. Here, I felt the presence of an intimacy that wanted to include me.

My ovaries, uterus, and vulva took hold of me and started operating independently. Forcing me to acknowledge the silent exchange through a language older than words in which my muscles and limbs seemed utterly fluent.

I felt as if my body was dissipating, liquefying, metamorphosing, birthing, ...

I felt sheer gratitude that I did not tame my senses and allowed the streaky Eros between my flesh and the flesh of the earth.

The landscape was breathing. Each flower, each leaf, each branch, each rock, carried a world within itself sustaining on a delicate cosmic equilibrium. Rocks, foliage, and corolla were chatting with one another and conferring with the blades of grass, passing down one thousand and one secrets and keeping them alive for centuries and for centuries to come.

The myriad flows and exchanges between the interconnected mycorrhizal networks penetrating the soil, the delicate yet resilient blades of grass touching the surface of rocks, the vine climbing on the trunk of a tree, the tree growing out from neatly arranged leaves, cranes hunting for food, ripples radiating at the intersection where earth and water meet, in those ripples the lotuses blossomed to compose a tightly woven cosmic web. These encounters, negotiations, and reciprocities were gradually intensifying in this little pocket of moss.

The leaves were sending ripples into the air in which the phoenix flew. The phoenix while flying whispered silently in my ear, that living, dying and transforming is a matter of indifference in the fabric of this community, where death is another kind of life.

The sap was now running in my veins.

How to Love a Tree, Chapter III
by Hira Nabi, 2022

ANNE RICHTER
The Sleep of Plants

TRANSLATED BY EDWARD GAUVIN

Anne Richter is a Belgian author, editor, and scholar. Her first collection, written at the age of fifteen, was translated as *The Blue Dog* by Alice B. Toklas, who praised her in the preface. In addition to her own fiction, she is known for editing an international anthology of female fantastical writers, *Le fantastique féminin d'Ann Radcliffe à nos jours* and writing essays about women writers and fantastical literature. In "The Sleep of Plants" a woman transforms into a plant in order to escape a humdrum, predictable life and seek the solitude she desires. It was first published in her collection *Les locataires* (*The Tenants*) in 1967.

"Slowing, we feel the pulse of things." —Henri Michaux, "La Ralentie"

She lived like a plant. The rhythms of her life were more vegetable than human. She was prone, periodically, to sliding slowly into sleep; she remained inactive, immobile, hands crossed on knees, head tilted slightly toward one shoulder, staring straight ahead. Sometimes it was a tiny thing. A wearied bee gone astray in a fold of curtain, patiently, haltingly making the climb, stopping to gather its strength. The bee would hunch up briefly before setting out again; the young woman waited for the moment when the insect would fall, at once wishing for and fearing it, so much a part of the creature's misery that her palms were moist. Or she would observe the exact whirl of dust motes in the light, between dresser and rug, finding secret calm in their constant movement. She followed water droplets gliding down gray panes, or would slip into one of her lengthy afflictions which never threatened her life, which she seemed to prolong for pleasure, from which she returned unhurriedly, eyes widened, a blue tinge to her skin, as if dazzled by the light upon leaving a cave.

* * *

She sank into utter solitude, surrounding herself with a rampart of silence. In these moments, her thoughts were vague, yet followed a precise path. With a spider's patience, she forced herself from behind half-closed eyelids to catch, unawares, things as she felt they must be. This required total stillness, arduous efforts of concentration. Meticulously, she repeated everyday words until they lost their usual meaning. *Spoon, spoon*, she would say, softly and stubbornly. She would polish the word, handling it almost absent-mindedly, yet taking care to treat it as respectfully as she could, never to consider it and see only usefulness. Little by little, it lost all consistency. Then began the meticulous work of a watchmaker. She persisted cautiously, decanted it, slowly breathed new life into the word. Sometimes she saw it come round, get back on its feet; then she would discover an entirely new meaning. She called this undressing words.

* * *

One day, she got engaged. Her fiancé was a likable young man. Sundays they often went for walks in the countryside. They trod carefully, hand in hand, along meadows and hedges. They spoke of this and that, without passion or impatience. One morning, George wanted to show her a place he'd found. They packed a lunch and set out. It was unusually warm. All the trees were in bloom, and the grass was tall in the fields. "There it is!" cried George. "Let's run for it!" They both broke into a sprint, and the young woman flew through the grass, laughing and waving her arms, displaying an unusual vitality. She reached the first trunk, and threw her arms around it; her fiancé caught up and kissed her on the mouth. The woods before them were split between sunlight and shadow. But suddenly she felt faint, and her hands gripped the bark. The young man was worried, surprised.

"Oh, it's nothing," she said.

She sat down in the grass and leaned her head against the trunk. Then she went pale, smoothed her dress, and glanced anxiously at her fiancé,

"What a pretty place!" she said.

But *le déjeuner sur l'herbe* was ruined.

They stopped going for walks. Her fiancé tried to drag her along, but she stubbornly refused, pleading fatigue. Around this time, she did in fact suffer from inexplicable spells of weariness. She was sorry, in all her immobility, that she couldn't sink roots. Bore into the ground for good, surround herself with a quiet cloud of light like those around pines or over certain shrubs in summer. But she had to get up from her chair, go here, go there. She did violence to herself speaking, moving, and afterwards fell back trembling, mouth dry, dying of thirst like a plant denied water.

The activity around her seemed less comprehensible than ever: needless commotion, futile chaos. And yet the regular course of daily affairs troubled her. She furled her leaves, lived on nothing. She was like a cactus, skin tender behind protecting needles, needing little water and light to live.

She saw that, by dint of stillness and withdrawal, you felt yourself become the center of the world, the source of its movement. As a child, she'd played at becoming the center of the world, an extraordinary game she never tired of—secretly aware, perhaps, of its gravity and power. She would walk backward, head thrown back and gazing at the sky until she grew dizzy. That was what she wanted, for dizziness to make her see things differently, herself frozen and the earth yawing, the sun and the clouds whirling about. Or else, sitting in a moving train, feeling the coarseness of the seat cushion beneath her palms, aware of the cadenced pace of travel in every part of her body, the train car stinking of cold ash, wet clothes, and smoke, she would scrutinize the white square of window, and suddenly the world would begin to change. The train had stopped, in the corner of her window she'd watch all the people walking, the meadows leaping past, the fleeing sky, slashed in its flight by taut telephone wires.

This state of grace almost always ended soon. The world grew still again, and her train car clattered along God knew where. Bitterness flooded her; disgust. She believed herself the only living person in a dead world shaken by sound and fury, till the day she understood: in motionlessness, movement found its source. She decided to fall silent, and in silence, animate the world.

* * *

This is what she did: she found a giant stoneware pot, a great bag of humus. She stepped into the basin, covered her legs in a blanket of earth. She vanished up to her hips. How good it felt! Never had she known such ecstasy. She was back in her element. From the depths of herself rose a silence. Still, a certain nervousness persisted, a tingle at the end of her fingers, toes, like expectation. *I'll get used to it*, she thought, wiggling her toes.

But there was a knock at the door; what would she tell her mother? The door opened and their eyes met. What grief in her mother's gaze!

"I always expected the worst from you, but not this—not this!"

"Look, I've always given in, but this time, your tears are wasted!"

In fact, things stayed much the same. After the initial shock, the usual routine set in. She'd never taken up much space in family life. From now on, she took up none at all. An empty chair at dinner was pushed to a corner. A vacant bed was moved to the attic. Clothes were given to the poor. Not once did her mother lift her gaze to the heavy basin upstairs. She vacuumed around it, cleaned the rug without comment, dusted quickly, her face expressionless. Maybe she hoped, by denying her daughter light, to see her wither and die. But plants are hardy. They have all the time in the world, and a gift for frugality.

When her fiancé came to see her, he didn't know what to say. He raised the blinds. She looked pale, her eyes ringed. Her arms hung slack at her sides like dead branches; her neck bowed beneath the moss of her hair. She gazed at him, not without a certain annoyance in her eyes: had his movements always been so brusque? She couldn't recall suffering from them before.

"You always said you wanted me to be happy," she murmured. "Probably you never noticed I was unhappy? This had to happen sooner or later. Isn't it better that it happened before we got married? You're still free now. Don't worry about hurting me."

George tried to take her hand, but it was so cold! As if blood were, ever so slowly, receding from it.

"How can you talk like that? Don't you know I love you? I would've died for you. But I can see that doesn't mean a thing to you; you're deliberately destroying yourself. What can I give you now?"

Despite everything, she was touched. But she was tired. The darkness had been a terrible ordeal for her. She turned her faded eyes to the sun, made an effort to speak.

"You're generous, George. There's something you can do for me, if you want. My mother won't admit it, but I know she wants bring things to an end as soon as she can. But I need food! Bring me things to eat and drink."

She was still a bit of a carnivore. Her fiancé brought her flies, mosquitoes, sometimes spiders. She swallowed them whole, hurriedly, craning her neck forward, snapping at them with sudden movements of her jaw. It was a peculiar sight, which her fiancé had a hard time watching. He turned discreetly away. But she soon lost her taste for meat. All that remained was a yearning for pure water, a dream of springs. Her ideas took the shape of leaves. Vague desires for silence. She spoke less and less. A bit embarrassed by her muteness, the fiancé spoke for them both.

One day he said, "If you'd wanted. Ania …"

But he didn't finish his sentence. He saw quite well that she no longer wanted a thing. In fact, she no longer even needed his presence. She possessed it forever, behind closed eyes. But he was still talking. They were all talking. How badly she wanted to drive off this insufferable swarm of words, as if waving away harmful insects!

Downstairs, they were saying, "Where's Ania?"

"Oh, in her room." "At a boarding house." "Traveling." "She's so shy, painfully shy!"

She was waiting for her roots. She shouldered the suffering of plants. The thirst of cut flowers torqueing their stalks toward the light. The moist dream of seaweed abandoned on the sand. The cold of rosebushes in November frost. The passing madness of indoor plants devouring walls and windows. The furious proliferation of exotic blossoms, brought over like slaves, strewing the four corners of the yard with the sinister fruit of their revolt. The sighs of men, stuck in the mud of futile acts.

Her fiancé conscientiously brought her water every day before going to work. He grew discouraged about talking, but she didn't notice. Sometimes he looked worried, but she was too preoccupied to notice. She was waiting. How long it was, the sitting still and waiting! We fill our days with distractions, but perhaps it would be better to be faithful to waiting—to wait without moving, speaking, lifting a finger, in a room bare as this one.

Her roots grew overnight. She felt them everywhere piercing the earth. What joy, alas, and what pain! She felt like she was traveling backward up the river of time. Odors assailed her, shifting essences. Her adolescence had an anxious scent, like bitter linden. Some had grown in the school playground where she'd always felt so bored. Her childhood smelled like sorb trees. She saw herself going down a curving path. A blackbird cackled from deep in a bush. Sorb apples lay bleeding in the grass. She squashed them underfoot. What world would spring forth when she rounded the bend? She advanced cautiously. With one final push, her roots punctured soil. Now she descended, heart pounding, toward an odor, the odor of the day she was born. Her birth had a dull smell, like the smell hanging over iron quarries. Her birth smelled like ferns. She saw a glittering fern, its crozier erect, scratch at the sky with its palm of light.

* * *

The next morning, her leaf hands were open. Her fiancé came to see her, looking vexed. He sat down beside her, head lowered.

"Look … I've given this a lot of thought. I think I owe it to you to tell you this. I've met someone … a young woman, the sister of someone at work. She's sweet, serious-minded … she looks like you a bit. You're the one who told me life goes on. But I can't just abandon you. Our lives are intertwined, Ania: do you want to come to our wedding, come live with us?"

A light breeze came in through the window. It caressed the trunk, played in the branches. The leaves up top bent forward a bit, in silent approbation. George bent over, lifted up the heavy stoneware basin. For a moment, the leaves grew flustered, shuddered. But they soon recovered their dreamy stillness. As Ania crossed the doorsill in the young man's arms, the mother, deep in her kitchen, closed her fist around a saucepan and turned her back to the couple.

* * *

George planted her in his yard, in the middle of the lawn. The roots breathed freely; she thanked him with a happy nod of foliage. One sunny morning not long after, he got married. The little pale-cheeked bride floated among the guests, light as a waterlily. There was dancing beneath leaves bathed in moonlight.

That summer, the tree put forth splendid blossoms.

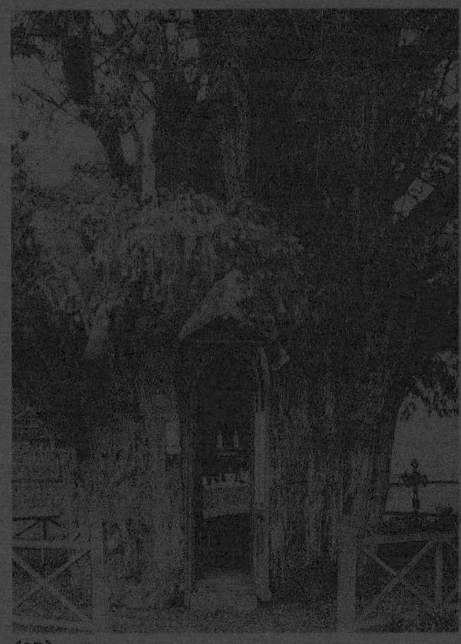

(15)

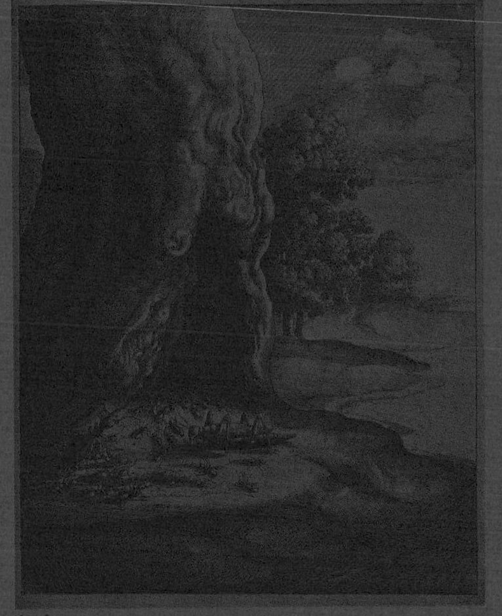

(16)

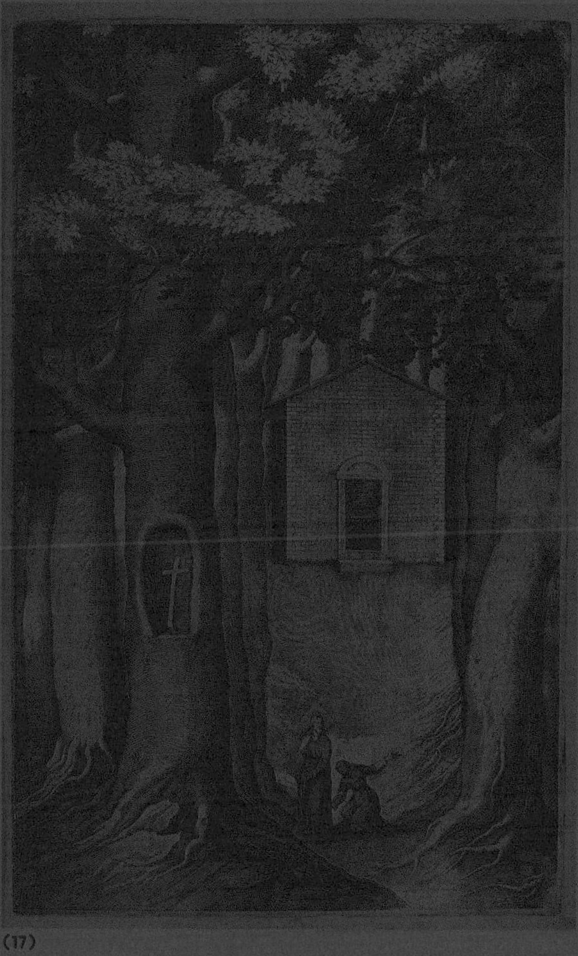

(17)

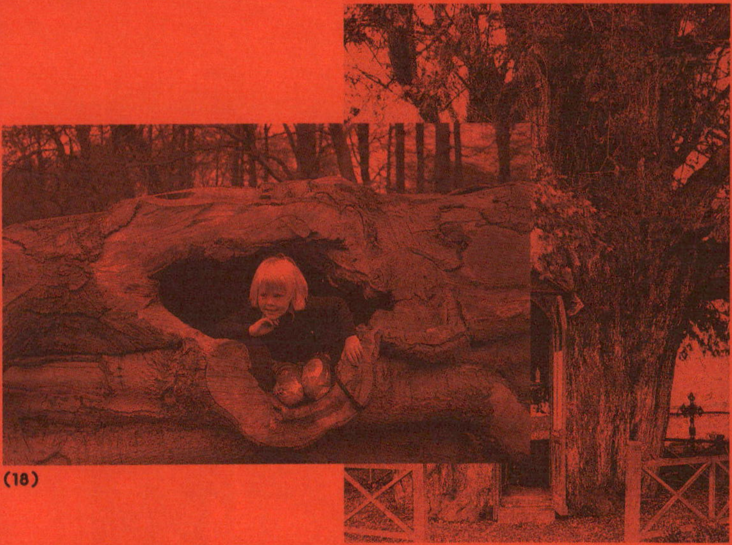

(18)

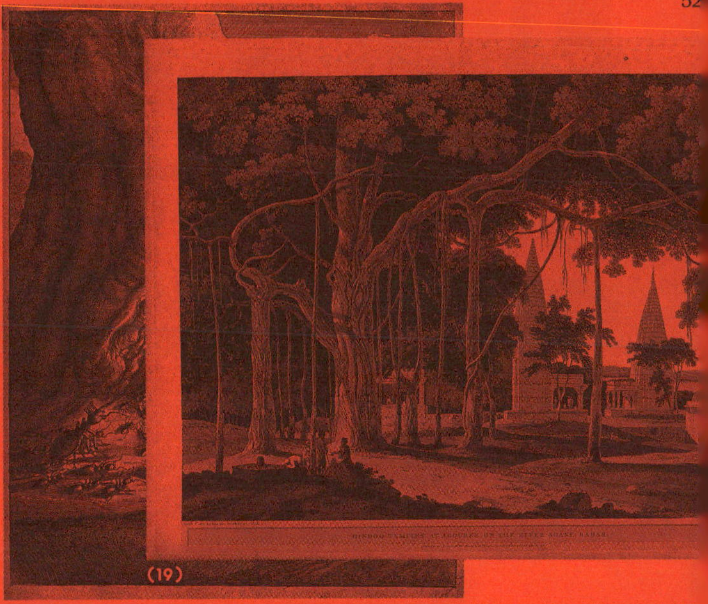

(19)

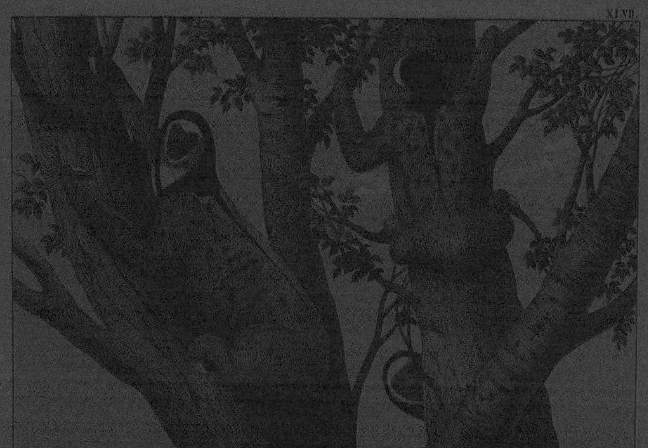

(20)

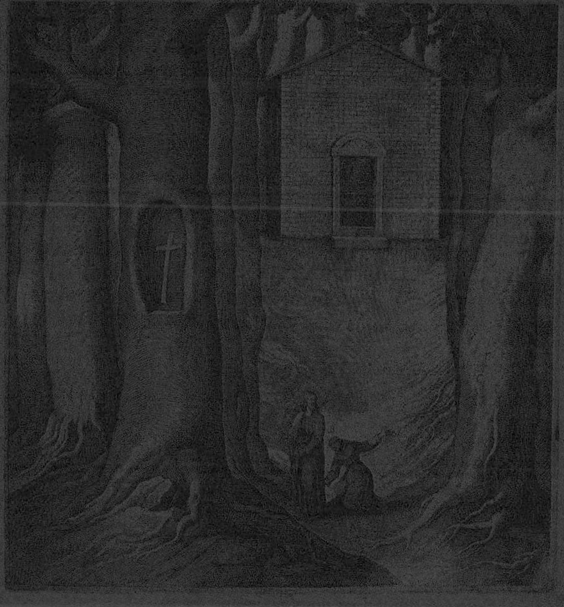

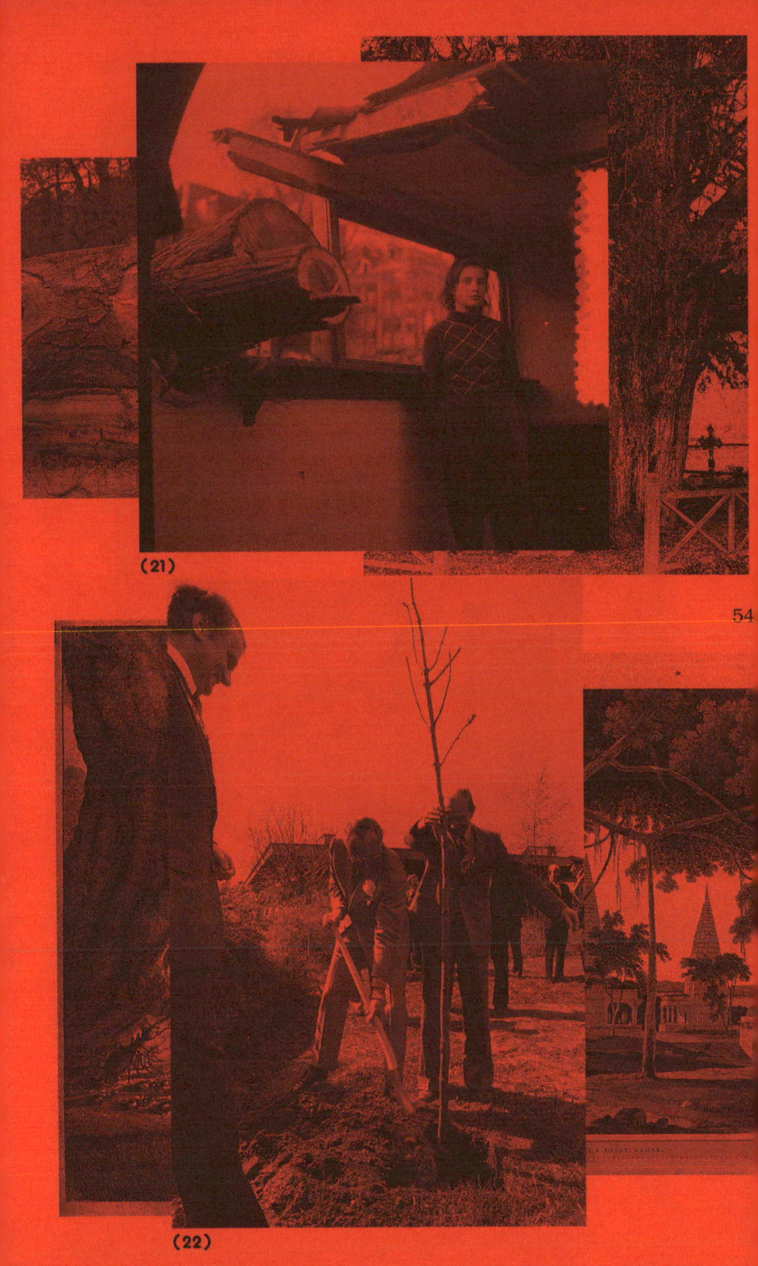

(21)

(22)

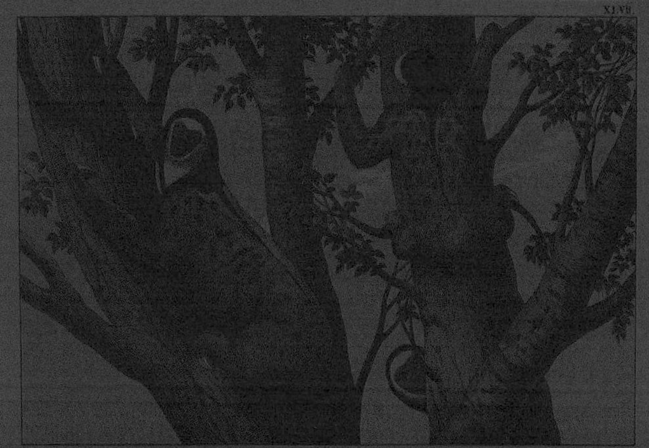

SOUTH AMERICA.
Yellow Throated Sloth.

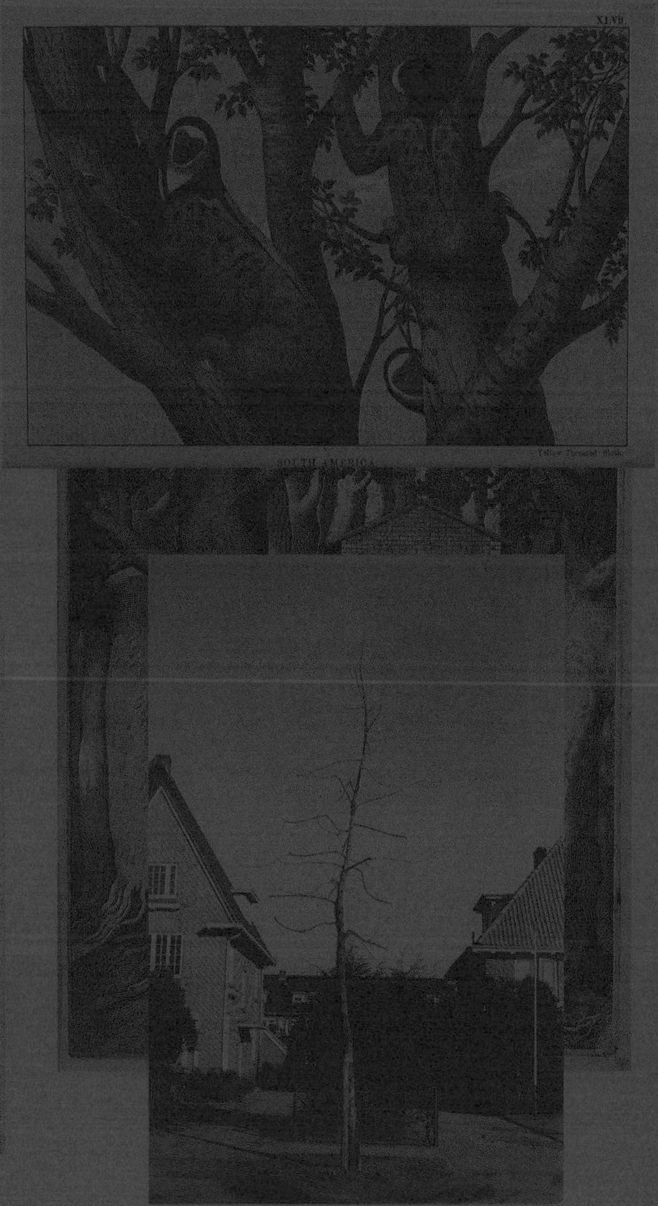

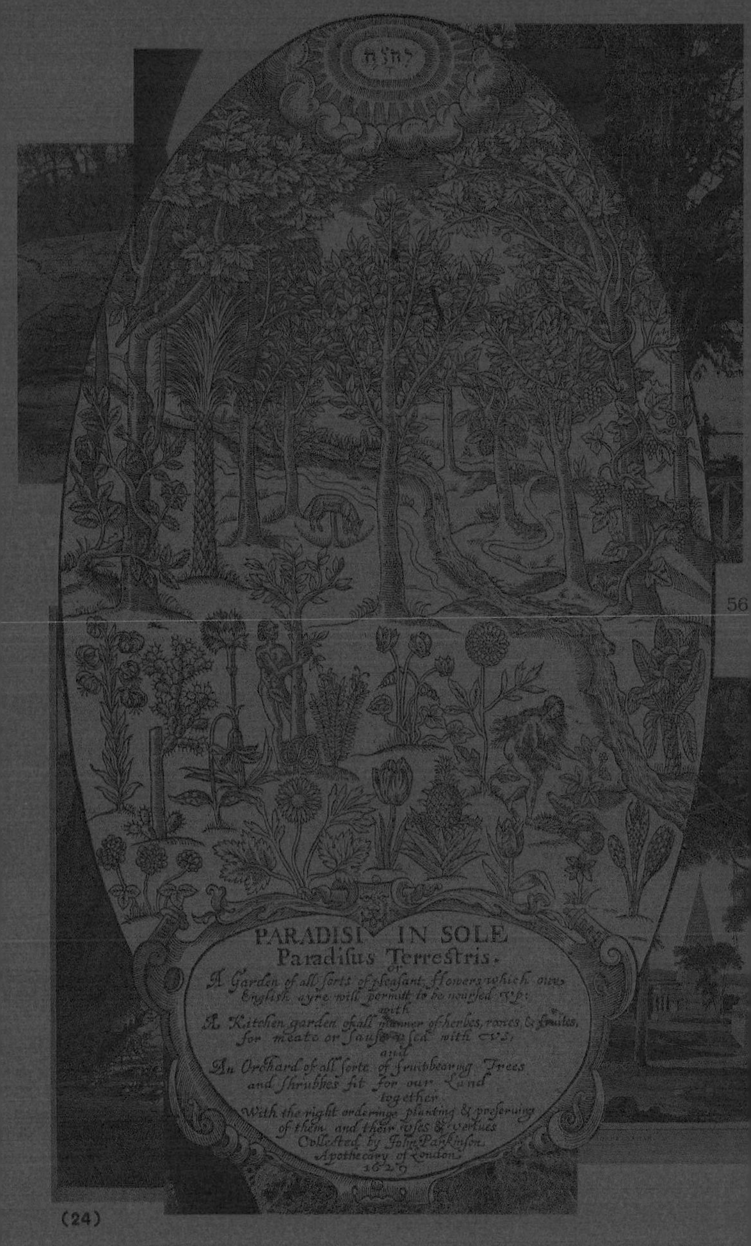
PARADISI IN SOLE
Paradisus Terrestris.
or
A Garden of all sorts of pleasant Flowers which our
English ayre will permitt to be noursed vp:
with
A Kitchen garden of all manner of herbes, rootes, & fruites,
for meate or sause vsed with vs;
and
An Orchard of all sorte of fruitbearing Trees
and shrubbes fit for our Land
together
With the right orderinge planting & preseruing
of them and their vses & vertues
Collected by John Parkinson
Apothecary of London
1629

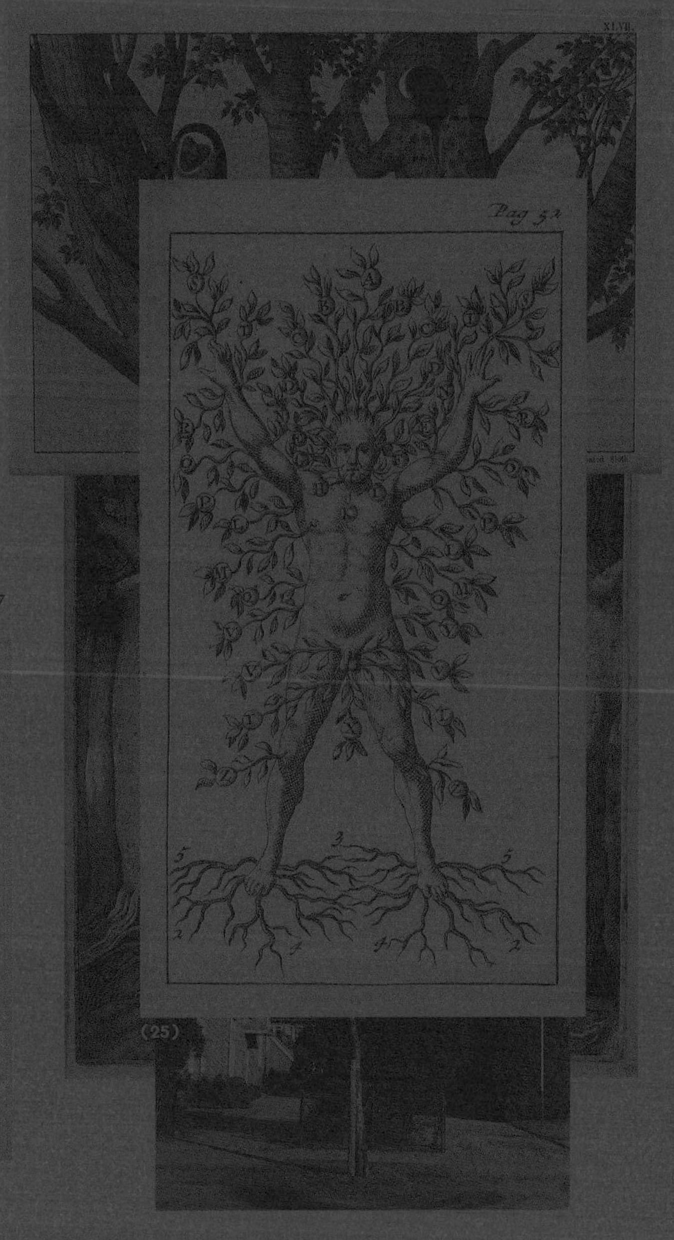
XLVII.
Pag. 52.
57
(25)

Birth Tree Ritual
by Jonmar van Vlijmen

In 2012, Ronald, my partner, and I moved to our current
home. A house with a large, overgrown back garden in
Amsterdam's Staatslieden neighborhood. The place is not
large, but the garden convinced us to move into social
housing close to the city center. As a result of moving into a
smaller house than before, we had to be strict in selecting
which things could move with us. While thinning out our book
collection, we came across a book I inherited from my grandmother as a teenager. Until then, I had never really placed
much value on its contents. Nonetheless, as one of the few
tangible memories of my grandmother, the book *Elsevier's
Guide to Wild Vegetables, Herbs, and Fruits* has followed me on
my journey since her passing.

When I encountered the book in preparation for the move,
my attention was drawn to little sheets sticking out between
the pages with small improvements to the recipes she used
in her kitchen. Leafing through the actively used book, it
struck me that it contained a chapter with stories about the
cultural and culinary significance of weeds, which our new
backyard was full of. This finding gave me a completely
different perspective on 'weeds'.

My perspective on plants came largely from my studies in
landscaping, a program in the late nineties that introduced
me to several thousand plant species that could be utilized
in a human-centered habitat. However, this heirloom of my
grandmother introduced me to other perspectives on the
weeds in the backyard of our new home. It led to a quest for

a different relationship with the plants around me that still keeps me engaged every day and is an integral part of my personal life and my artistic practice.

Our daughter was born on February 2, 2022, and she will eventually inherit my Grandmother's book. When she turned one year old, we celebrated her birthday with a birth tree ritual, collectively with her two mothers and guests. During this ritual, we planted a Ginkgo tree in a prominent spot in our garden on top of our daughter's placenta. We applied crushed eggshells from the chickens living in our garden in a circle around the placenta that function as a gestational gift to the tree we had chosen to feed on the temporary organ that nourished our daughter in the womb. These calcium-rich shells, in return, form a nutritional component of the ecosystem of our garden and, as such, introduce the Ginkgo to the different actors as part of the created family home. Since then, the organ has become part of the ecosystem of the Ginkgo tree and all the living organisms that keep the soil around it moving.

When I look at the tree now -- from the dining table where I eat with our daughter, draw 'speculative ecosystems,' or write -- I realize that my relationship with the garden has changed. Now that the placenta has been incorporated into the ecosystem of our garden, I feel a deep connection between my body and all the organisms that have, like me, incorporated this organ into their metabolism. There is no longer a distinction between the garden and my body; they have become one and are constantly connected. We breathe each other out and into existence. The Ginkgo tree has now joined our family like an honored member and is infinitely connected to us through the garden, inseparable from our household and central to our lives. Through the ritual, the garden is forever marked as an origin for our daughter. Wherever her journey may take her, there is always a place to come home to, thanks to Grandma's book.

<u>INSTRUCTIONS</u>

o Start collecting eggshells during your pregnancy.
   They contain valuable minerals and calcium that can
   contribute to the health of your garden. Dry the eggshells
   and pulverize them, then store them in a sealed jar;

o store the placenta in your freezer until a day before
   planting the birthing tree;

o prepare a tree of choice for its new habitat and imagine
   how it becomes part of your family by caring for its roots
   with nutrition and water;

o dig a pit with a depth depending on the root ball of the
   chosen tree, with a diameter of 100 cm;

o dig a round trench in the pit with a diameter of 80 cm;
   this trench will be filled with the collected eggshells;

o make a bed for the placenta by pushing some earth aside.
   You can choose to place precious memories, such as a
   lock of hair or a piece of umbilical cord, before putting
   down the placenta;

o place the placenta and cover with a generous layer of
   garden soil;

o place the tree and fill the hole with the remaining
   garden soil, and water generously;

o the tree will appreciate it when you regularly reflect
   on the moment it was added to your garden's ecosystem.
   A year after planting, you can ask the tree to take
   cuttings and share the birth tree with family members
   and friends.

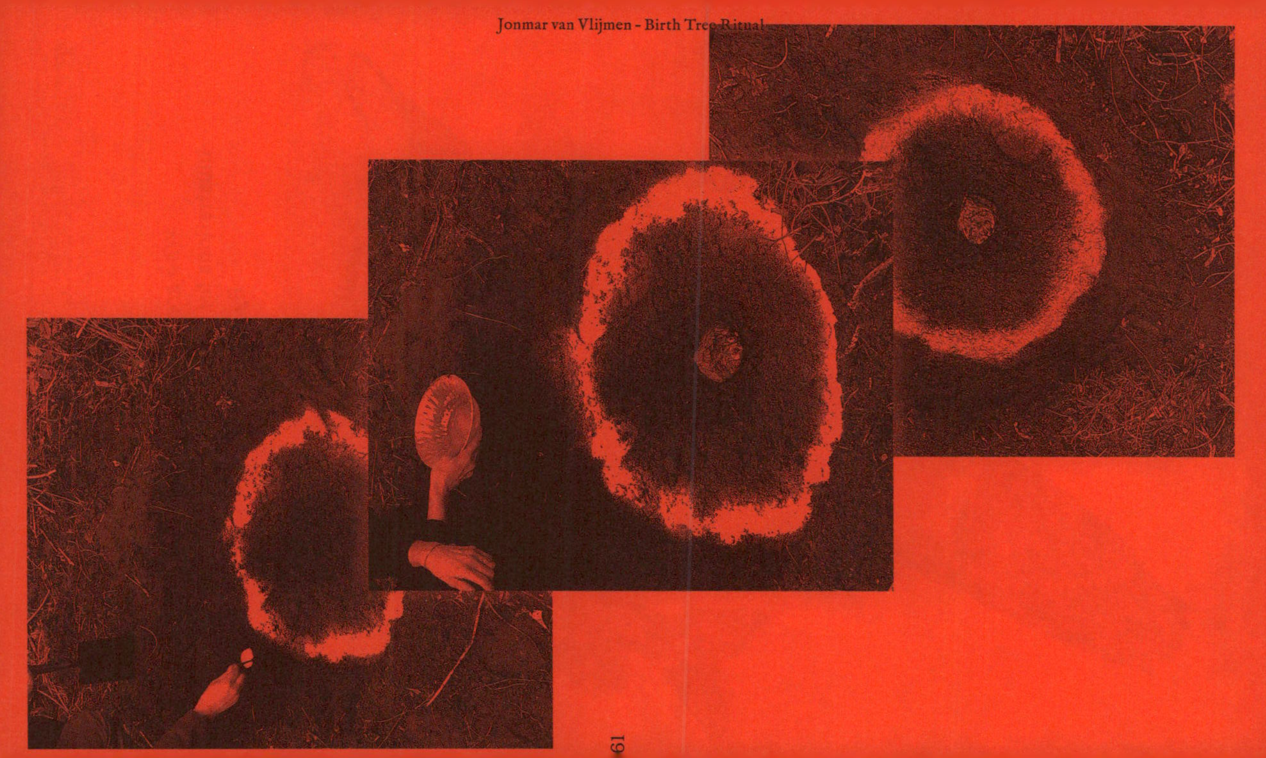

Who are you? (Vilka är ni?)
Illustrations for theatre performance, 2018
By Ingela Ihrman

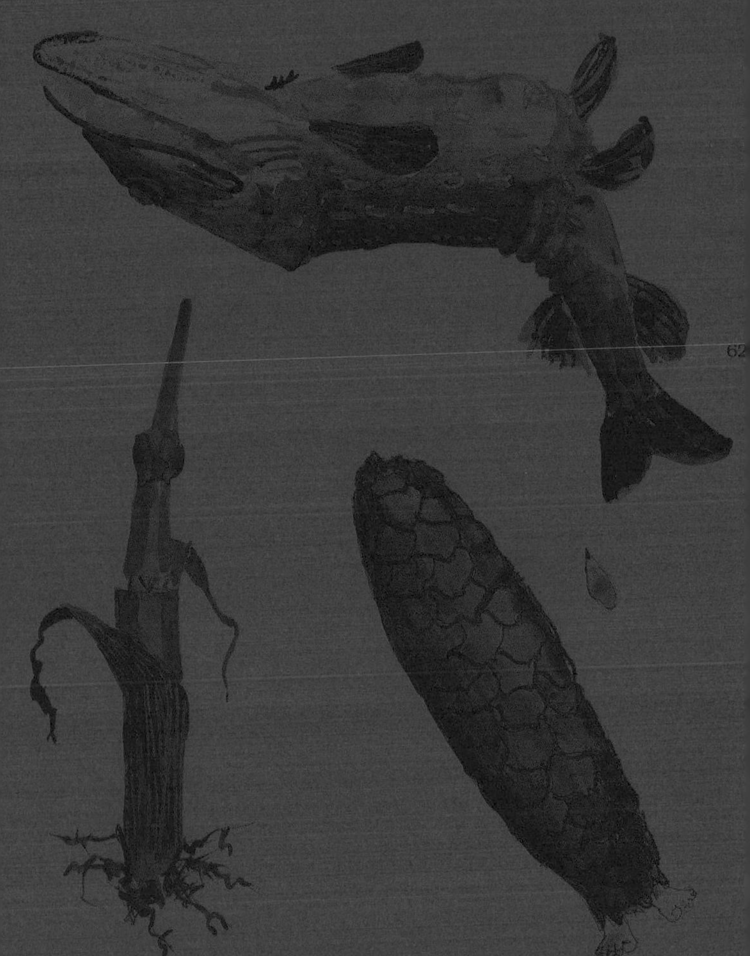

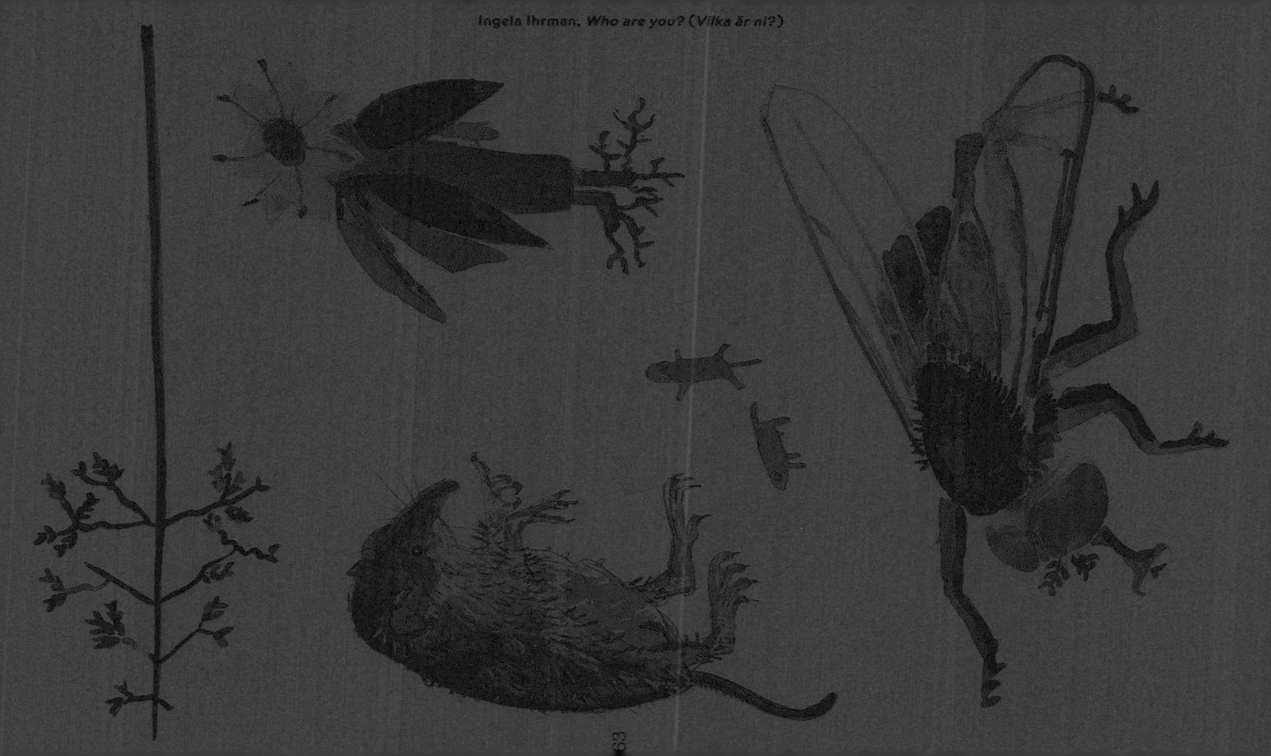

Ingela Ihrman. Who are you? (Vilka är ni?)

SILVER MAPLE HEEMRAADSSINGEL
BY ALICE LADENBURG

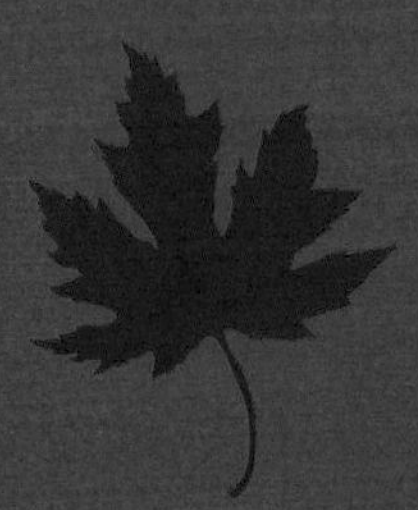

Acer saccharinum | ID: 89321   10/11/2020 | 10:32

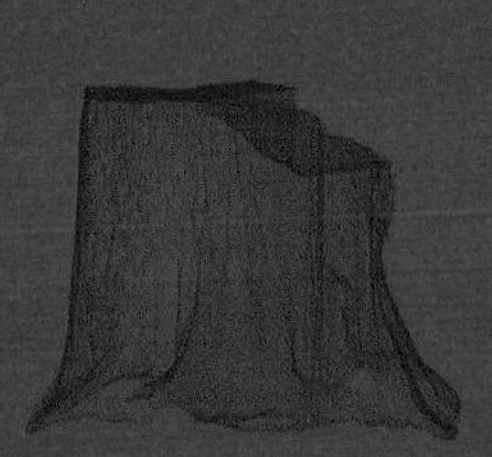

17/12/2020 | 17:47   27/05/2024 | 13:52

28th July 2020
09:10

A blanket of leaves, clinging to its trunk like Ivy. Branches fork confidently into the sky, spreading over this long wide green channel, a peaceful city slice. Red t-shirt, green t-shirt strutting men pass. A lady power-walks satisfyingly across the gravel. A thump of music somewhere away. Honking geese and a wind rustle through leaves. A tram whistle passing, stopping, continuing. A neutral breeze.

LUIS' OAK TREE
BY BÁRBARA SÁNCHEZ BARROSO
an excerpt from a work-in-process novel

Next to the road to Talavera, at the entrance to the highway that leads to Cáceres, there is a green piece of land that belongs to Villanueva. The terrain is uneven and uniform, a gravel path crosses it, and leaving behind the road and the constant noise of cars and trucks passing by, it is a place full of tall grass and shrubs, such as thistles, wheat, broom and oleander.

Among them grow thistle mushrooms and wild asparagus. As you climb the hill you can see the bridge of Talavera in the distance, so high that it can be seen from any place higher than 5 meters above ground level.

But what is most striking about this place is an oak tree. A large and wide oak rests on top of the hill and is surrounded only by olive trees around it. A little further down there are 3 burnt cypress trees that frame it when you look at it from a 90-degree angle between the road and the hill.

I see it from the road, when passing by car, entering the village. Its spreading branches greet you, displaying their exuberance.

Here some people come from the village to pick mush-rooms, they drive down following a dirt road that crosses the highway under a very narrow and high cement tunnel.

Today I have climbed this hill, stumbling over the over-turned stones that abound among the grass, like quartz, granite and limestone. This is a terrace, thousands of years ago this was a river.

After continuing to walk up the steep terrain I reach the oak tree and with effort I climb it, holding on to a branch. In the middle of the tree, where the trunks meet, a kind of nest opens up and welcomes you, becoming the perfect place to sit.

I sit comfortably, still gasping for breath, watching the branches, the trunks and their knots, how they split and as they move away from me these become smaller and more abundant, and hundreds, and then thousands of leaves appear.

It must be almost 6 p.m. now, it is December, the sun will disappear soon and the light turns yellow on only one side of the leaves, the other remains dark. I caress the bark of the tree and little pieces of bark remain in my hand, as if it were breaking, I feel its old age, its tiredness.

There is a trunk that stands out before all the others, it must be more than 2 meters high from the ground, and it is the one that catches my attention the most. It is robust and beautiful.

That's when I hear some branches breaking behind me and I see him. It's my uncle Luis, he's coming up the hill slowly. As he approaches I see his slow and tired step, his serious and stubborn countenance. I watch him without moving from my nest, from the oak tree and its branches that surround and hide me. He comes straight towards the oak, until he touches it and caresses it with one hand, carrying something in the other, what looks like a rope.

I know what he is going to do, I have heard it many times in conversations that have happened around me but in which I have not been a participant. I am 8 years old and I have not yet finished understanding those terms, then I am 20 and I hear it in comments made with choppy words. I am 30 and we no longer talk about the past, it's taken for granted that we know it. That which should not be named, that which cannot be said, something unpronounceable.

I watch him from above throw the rope against the branch, I close my eyes and only hear the sound of the rope rubbing against the bark and the bark peeling. The oak is tired. I open my eyes and I am here again, alone, with the pristine branches and the whole bark.

I jump down from the tree and caress that branch that I imagine was the chosen one and I feel peace, in the silence of nature broken only by the sound coming from the road. I walk down the hill at a fast pace, afraid that it might get dark, and look at the oak tree from below. I think of Luis' sense of aesthetics, I would choose her too, the tired oak alone on the hill surrounded by olive trees.

When I get to the gravel road I see his car, next to the cypress trees, I look inside and there is a piece of rope. I keep walking towards the village through the tunnel under the road and think about how I wish I could transport myself back to that moment. But no one ever told me anything else, only someone pointed to that oak tree and talked about the car down by the cypress trees, from the highway as we drove through it on the way to town, in between broken sentences about what should never have been done.

A DAY IN THE LIFE OF A TREE
BY INTERSPECIES LIBRARY (OSCAR SALGUERO)

SIDE B
[A Day in the Life of a Tree]
Just a year after the first Earth Day, Brian Wilson, co-founder of The Beach Boys, released *A Day in the Life of a Tree* (Surf's Up, 1971), a somber piece of experimental pop music sung from the perspective of a dying tree affected by pollution. "[It was] about the environment ... a tree thinking out loud (or thinking silently but singing out loud) about all the bad things that were happening to it."[1] Intuitive, tender, seeding, Brian's empathy grew arborescent. For acoustics, the sound designer suggested a wood pipe organ ("to represent the majesty of a tree"); for vocals, they used the band manager's test singing session as it carried the most emotion; for atmosphere, bird sounds were recorded in Brian's patio...

SIDE A
[trees: Pinus silvestris (Excerpt 48 hours)[2]]
In 2015, environmental scientists/artists Marcus Maeder and Roman Zweifel developed *treelab*, a project consisting of sonifying ecophysiological data and recording acoustic emissions in trees in Valais, Switzerland, a forest of Scots Pine trees. "This particular species is already at its physiological limit regarding drought and heat periods,... so parts of the forest are already dying."[3] *treelab*'s intention was to evoke a sonic, emotional, "all-encompassing experience from very different and complex data sets... of the life processes and environmental conditions of a tree that is under pressure from changing climatic conditions."[4]

We suggest playing tracks A and B simultaneously to
experience half-a-century of sonic kinship with trees.
To accompany the soundtrack, we invite you to browse
the following books:

- *Traducir un Bosque* (2021) by Santiago Morilla (ES)
- *Yaj Gotój A. Botánica de los Sueños* (2022)
  by Daniel Godínez Nivón (MX)
- *Die Bork-Bibliothek* (2023) by Nicole Brugger (CH)

1   Wilson, Brian; Greenman, Ben (2016). *I Am Brian Wilson:
    A Memoir.* Da Capo Press. pp. 156–157.
2   Maeder, Marcus. "Trees: Pinus Sylvestris."
    Journal for Artistic Research, November 8, 2016.
    https://www.researchcatalogue.net/view/215961/215962.
3   "Sound the Alarm: Data Sonification as a Tool for
    Climate Action." Ableton. Accessed June 10, 2024.
    https://www.ableton.com/en/blog/sound-the-alarm-data-
    sonification-as-a-tool-for-climate-action/.
4   Maeder (n 2).

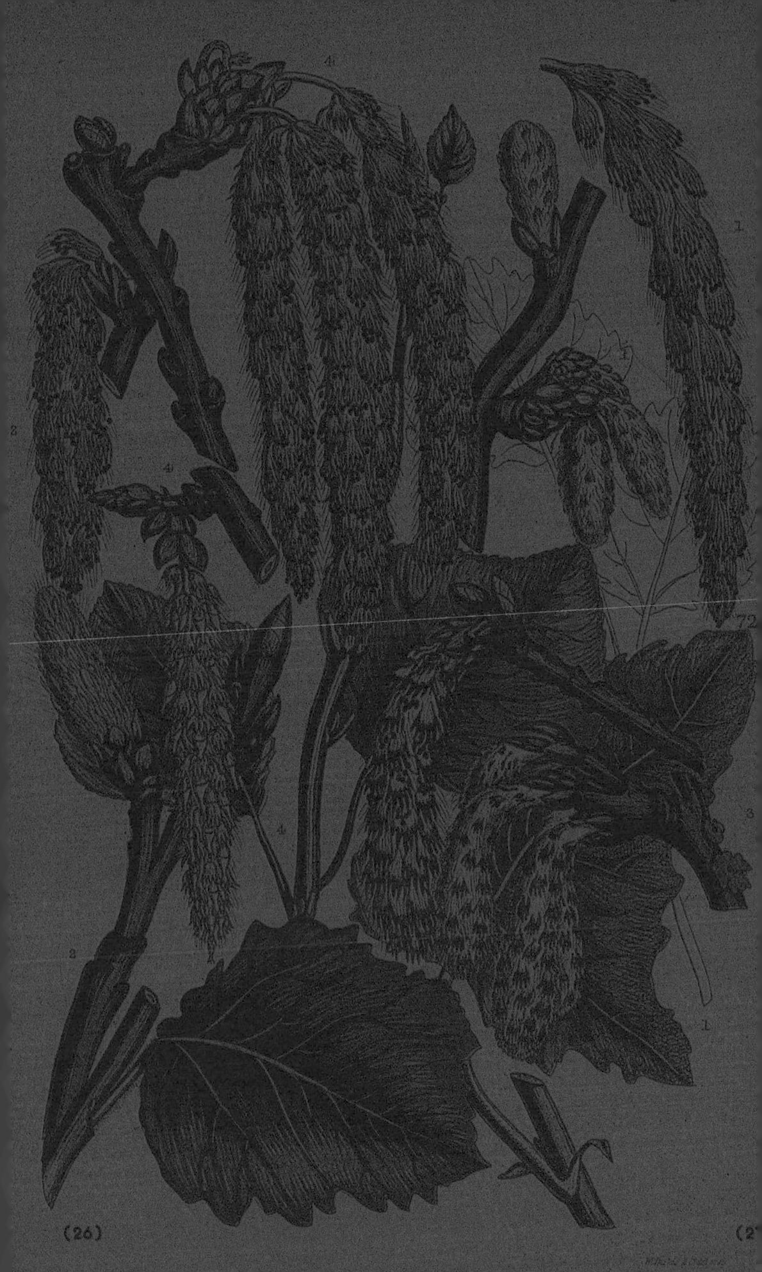

1
2
3
4

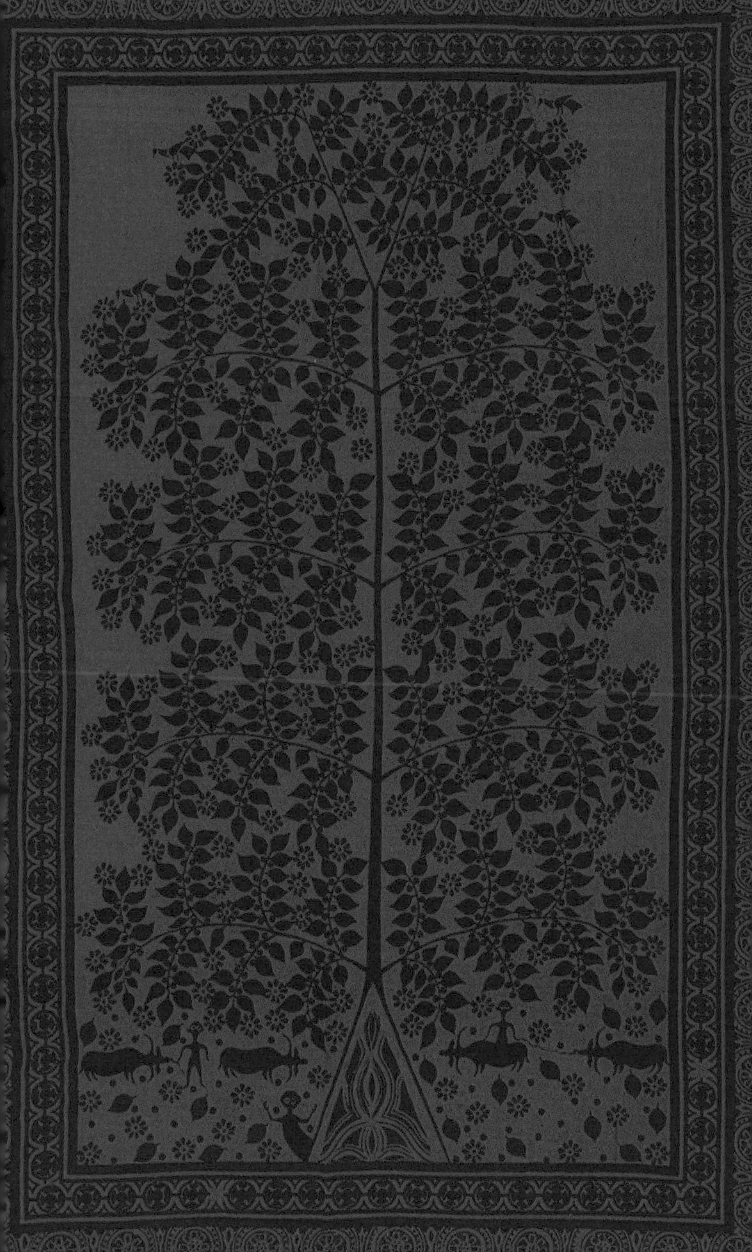

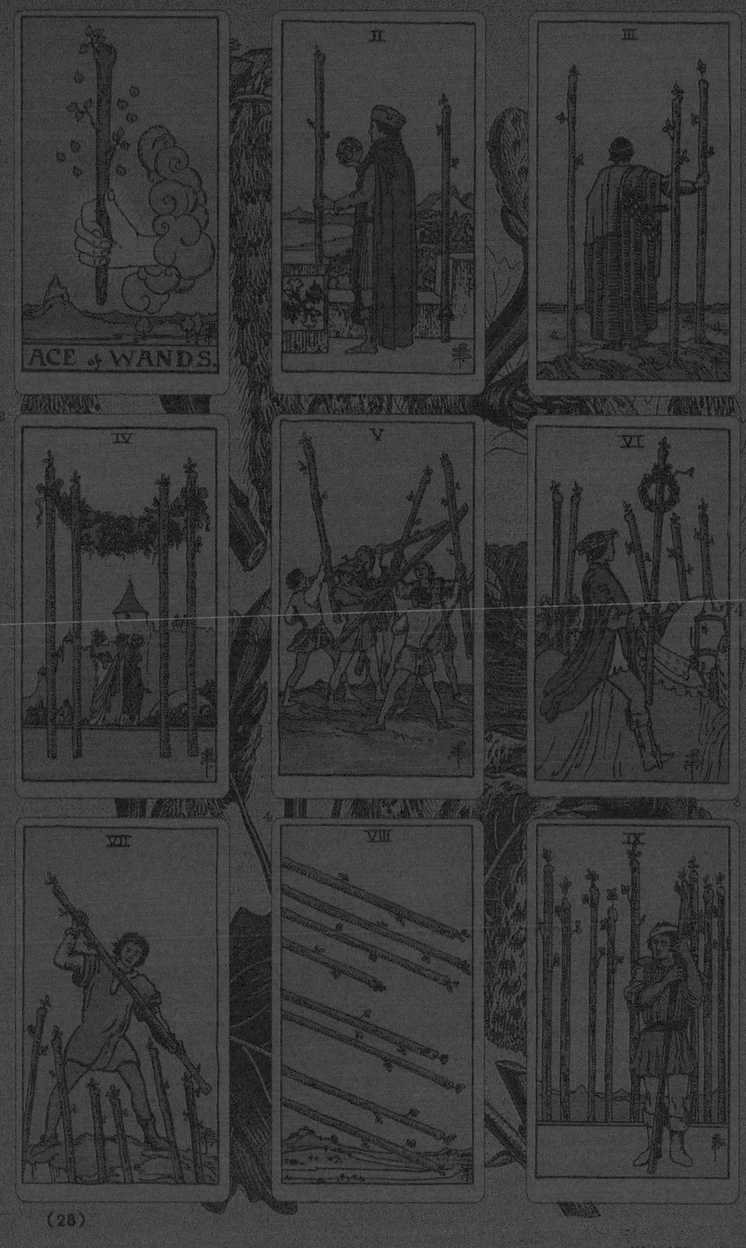

ACE of WANDS.
(28)

PAGE of WANDS.
KNIGHT of WANDS.
QUEEN of WANDS.
KING of WANDS

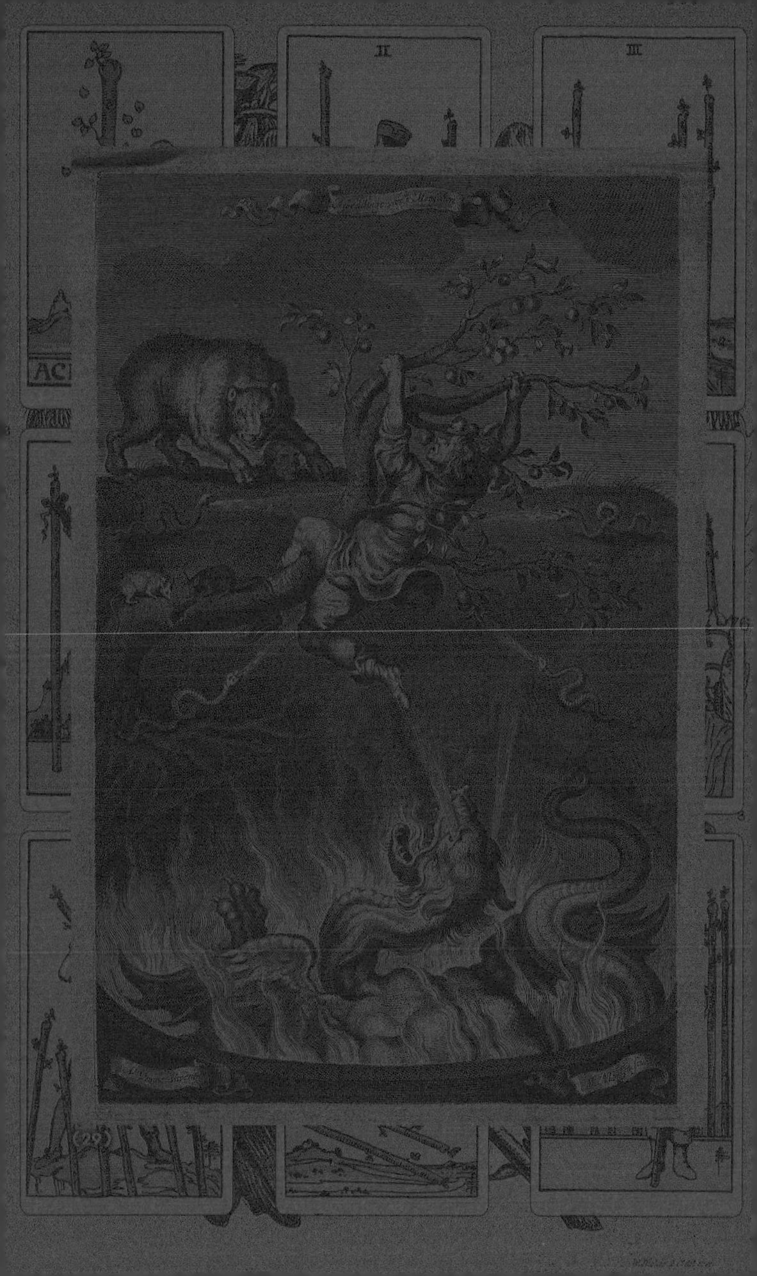

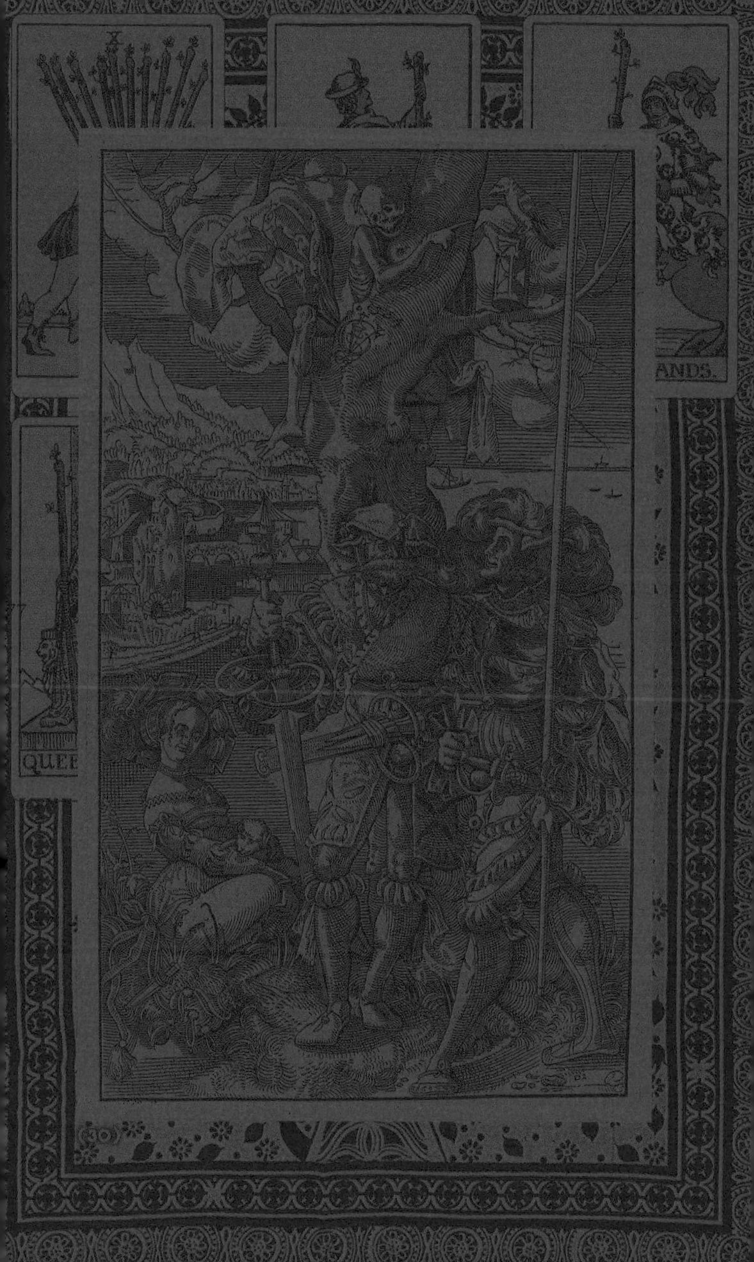
QUEE
ANDS.

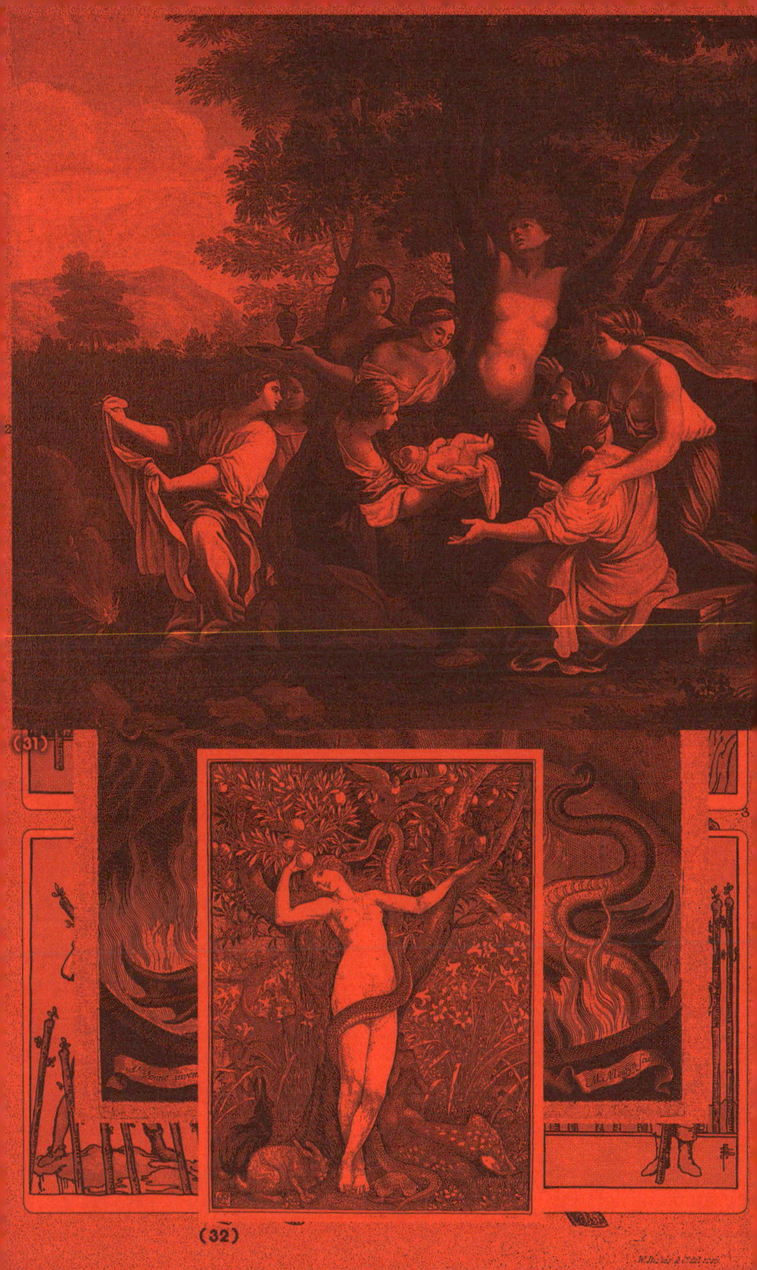
(31)
(32)
3

QUEE

Trails of a Tree
by Sanne Vaassen, 2015

"During one autumn, I collected all the
leaves of one tree and marked the pavement
where I collected them with a white marker.
The tiles were photographed, numbered,
and notated on a map."

Sonic Vaasseh Trailsofa Jsec

EVERYTHING GOES IN NATURE:
LEARNINGS FROM THE PLANT KINGDOM
BY CELINE BAUMANN

Plant kingdom is manifold: with an infinite variety of shapes, colours, textures, and smells, it is averse to resemblance. The origin of this extreme diversity results from evolution through sexual reproduction, allowing to adapt to ever changing weather, climate, and soil conditions. Sexual reproduction amongst trees and herbs is multifaceted and plants can be either male, female, hermaphroditic, or even all at once. While this fact is nowadays widely acknowledged, it caused at its discovery an uproar, challenging patriarchal ideas about procreation. To acknowledge the variety of reproduction behaviours in the plant kingdom, is to allow the emergence of an emancipated idea of nature, not as something separate and dominant, but as relational and queer. Lessons learnt from the plant kingdom may also apply to other fields, and accordingly guide us towards the creation of a more inclusive urban environment.

Reproduction in the plant world has the particularity, in contrast with animals, to be able to happen in two distinct ways: either sexually or vegetatively. Vegetative propagation is commonplace in the wild: strawberries shoot out new plants thanks to their runners, stinging nettle spreads via its rhizomatic root systems. It can also be induced artificially, and horticulturalists use techniques such as cutting, grafting, layering, or even tissue culture to multiply commercially houseplants and flowers purchased in garden centres. This manufactured botany is economically profitable as it breeds plants quickly but has the disadvantage to come at the cost of diversity, as vegetative propagation produces plant replicas that all carry an identical genetic material and are de facto clones. Sexual reproduction, in contrast, allows plants to evolve by selecting a balance of the most favourable genetic characteristics of the parent plants. This is a slow and demanding process, yet necessary to allow the mutations that inevitably happen during growth and are vital to adapt to and often-changing environment – and crucially nowadays to global heating. Sexual reproduction happens thanks to the pollination process, this non-hierarchical relationship based on an exchange with bees, insects or birds, and involves either male, female or hermaphroditic flowers, whose sexual organs can be arranged according to a wide variety of patterns.

Some species carry plants that can only be either exclusively male or exclusively female, what botanists call 'dioecy'. The yew (*Taxus baccata*), for instance, carries either only male or only female flowers. After pollination, the male flowers are shed while the female ones turn into a red berry-like structure, the aril, whose ornamental qualities are cherished by gardeners. This feature can also evolve with time, as proven by the oldest male yew of the Royal Botanical Garden of Edinburgh, which happened to develop a branch carrying female flowers. Other examples of dioecious plants include gingko, stinging nettle, kiwis, hop and asparagus. Other species carry separate male and female cones or flowers on the same plant, known to botanists as 'monoecy'. The Scots Pine (*Pinus sylvestris*) carries both male and female cones on distinct parts of the same plant. The male cones are recognizable thanks to the conspicuous yellow colour of their pollen. Once fertilised, the juvenile female cones turn into mature ones carrying the tree's naked seeds. Many conifers are monoecious and other examples include deciduous species such as plane tree, hornbeam, alder, birch, hazel, and walnut.

Dioecy and monoecy are actually rather archaic mechanisms of sexual reproduction and they were later in the evolution enhanced by a novel feature: hermaphroditism. Hermaphroditic plants gather both male and female cells within a single organ, what botanists describe as 'perfect' flowers. Most of the plants we know today are hermaphroditic, and the longlist includes lime tree, horse chestnut, magnolias, most fruit trees, vegetables, and ornamental plants. The sexual characteristics of plants are also not fixed, and they may also evolve with time and depending on factors like age or environmental conditions. A hermaphroditic plant can also carry solely male or solely female flowers, or both, a male tree can suddenly produce female flowers... Everything goes in nature.

The first known reference of plant sexuality in the western world appeared in antiquity, when the philosopher Aristotle audaciously compared plants to upside-down animals. According to him, roots were comparable to the mouth as a nurturing organ, twigs to legs, and consequently sexual organs should also be present on the plant structure above ground. The philosopher's intuition was not scientifically pursued until the end of the 17th century, when natural scientist Camerarius wrote the first modern publication on plant sexual reproduction, later used by the botanist Linnaeus as a basis for his own work on classification. This was actually not an easy recognition, as the sole idea of plant sexuality challenged religious and patriarchal views of the time of nature as devoid of what was considered as immoral behaviours. Subsequent discussions lasted for almost a hundred years until, in the late 19th century, the scientific community ultimately reached a consensus on the true existence of plant sexuality. This realisation came uncannily late in the history of natural sciences, when we think that sexual reproduction in the animal world had been known since antiquity. Hand-pollination has in fact been commonplace ever since the beginning of agriculture – although it was not acknowledged as such. Artworks found in modern Iraq show Assyrian arborists manually fertilising the female flowers of date palms with male ones to produce the sweet edible fruit (like yews, date palms are dioecious and can only be either male or female). Hand-pollination had also been used for horticultural purposes since ancient times by plant breeders in order to create new varieties of flowers. This art reached an apex during the 17th century Netherlands, when florilegium paintings depicted the abundance of shapes and colours produced by tulip breeders. Intense speculation over the exchange of the flower bulbs led to what is now known as the Tulip Mania, when the price of coveted tulip bulbs increased one hundredfold within a few years, leading to the world's first recorded economic bubble and ensuing first world's financial crash.

The diversity of the natural world is remarkable, and challenges prejudiced ideas of what is considered as being natural, i.e. proper. Lessons learnt from the plant kingdom may also apply to other fields, and as a landscape architect I am interested to investigate how this can apply to the design of open spaces. The success of public demonstrations like Women's Marches and Pride

Parades shows a rising demand from citizens to transgress patriarchal and heteronormative conformism. The public realm is a prominent space of expression for civil society and requires to be placed under scrutiny.

Within the city of Basel, where I live, around one hundredth of all streets and squares are named after people. The namesakes include historical and political luminaries, influential families, cultural actors, and mythological figures. Just about a tenth of the spaces are named after women, and out-of-the-closet gays are simply absent. This situation is widespread and, to highlight this issue, feminist and queer groups throughout Europe are undertaking bottom-up activism, renaming to their likings the public realm in cities like Geneva, Paris and Amsterdam. Some governments are hearing them: in tribute to the Stonewall riots, for instance, Paris renamed a series of squares and streets after local and international queer personas, including the transgender writer and resistance fighter Ovida Delect, the Holocaust survivor Pierre Seel, and the politician and activist Harvey Milk.

Other insights of gender-biased public spaces are visible in the range of freely accessible recreational available in squares and gardens. A study conducted in Geneva reveals that city subsidised sport resources are allocated to men in more than two-thirds of cases, and that they too often favour power and stamina over dexterity and non-normative bodies. Facilities for strength-based recreation like skateboarding or urban fitness, which are conventionally regarded as masculine activities, are widespread, while amenities addressing agility and team sports such as badminton or volleyball, which are generally feminine-coded, are underrepresented in many public spaces.

Those patriarchal values are also permeating other fields of public space and maybe more surprisingly, are also recognizable in the choice of trees used to plant our streets. Urban trees are a key feature of European cities, adorning the cityscape with their leafy presence, usually planted linearly to emphasise the geometry of a pedestrian axis or border traffic-heavy avenues or boulevards. Limes and planes are some of the most popular European alley trees, followed closely by horse chestnuts and maples. They provide a vast array of ecological services to citizens: they shade the streets, contribute to a pleasing micro-climate thanks to evapo-transpiration, produce oxygen and clean the air by collecting dust on their foliage. They also gulp excess rainwater and serve as hosts for many varieties of birds and insects. When planted over a larger territory, they act as valuable agreement and precious ecological corridor, one of the most famous examples of such an urban corridor to this date remains the Boston Emerald Necklace from Frederick Law Olmsted.

The range of challenges facing street trees is also fierce: they should be able to grow in reduced tree pits with compacted soil, resistant to air pollution, drought, excess water, be easily trimmed to accommodate traffic, especially large trucks, streetlights, and tramway catenaries. In order to fulfil all those demands, some tree species were even engineered especially for that purpose, such as the London Plane (*Platanus × hybrida*), which is a cross breed between an oriental plane and an American Sycamore. This London landmark is tolerant to root compaction and air pollution, resists wind and drought well, making it a very proper and resistant urban tree.

Hygiene and low maintenance are also decisive factors for the choice of the appropriate street tree. The chosen species should not exhale unpleasant smells or produce large fruits, which are regarded by municipalities as a source of extra workload and a health hazard, as falling fruits may render the pavement slippery and attract unsolicited insects such as wasps and flies. When available, the male tree is too often favoured to the female one. This applies to species like poplar, ash, willow or gingko, the latter female specimen producing fruit carrying an acrid smell usually considered as highly unpleasant. Those choices have regrettable unintended consequences, as the male trees are the ones producing pollen, which is cause to many spring allergies. This also poses the question of the place of production and reproduction within our cityscapes. Why do we revere flowers, while we forbid fruits? Is the only purpose of urban trees to be ornamental?

The gap between ornamental and horticultural varieties does not need to be so sharp and hopeful examples show how (re)production can find its place in our metropolitan environments. One of the most hopeful examples to that regard is the city of Seville in Spain, whose streets are bordered by Bitter Orange trees (*Citrus × aurantium*). In the spring, the city is filled with the fragrance of orange blossoms, while the plump fruits adorn the autumn and winter months. The bitter taste is though not favoured by the Spaniards and once harvested, bitter oranges are shipped to England where they are turned into a sweet-sour marmalade, to the delight of the Britons.

Climate change is demanding city planners and landscape architects all around the world to unsettle their habits and review the traditional assortment of urban trees. Species like beech, spruce, or birch suffer tremendously from increased heat and lack of water. This is a tragedy, as many trees will not survive our heated future, but it is also the opportunity to broaden our palette with species that are not only resistant to global warming but can also play a role in feeding our cities. The Sweet Chestnut (*Castanea sativa*) for instance, is a tree originating from the Mediterranean area known to be heat tolerant. Its fruits, the chestnuts, are also a valuable source of carbohydrate and can be eaten roasted, turned into flour, or candied. The plantation of such species as alley trees offers the opportunity to shape an urban future where fructification and reproduction find a room of their own, allowing the emergence of a cityscape which is not only ornamental and fragrant, but also palatable.

Queering the public realm—that is, fostering a diversity of genders expression—can address both plants and people. Unseal the soil; make it porous and permeable to create a welcoming ground for all. Grant free spaces for roots to grow and communities of humans as well as nonhuman to mingle. By exploring the power of trees, shrubs, flowers and herbs as a source of inspiration, we can find alternatives to the way we design and act in order to shape truly inclusive metropolitan ecosystems.

Acorn / An Oak Tree / Octavia E.
by Müge Yilmaz

Octavia E. Butler wrote *The Parable of the Sower* in 1993.
I was 8 years old. The protagonist of Butler's novel, Lauren
Oya Olamina was not born yet. In the novel, the community
led by Lauren has a tradition of planting an oak tree for each
person that passes away.

In 2019 I brought an acorn found in the town of my grandmother, Kandira, back to Amsterdam and put it in the fridge.
I was 34 years old. The average life of an oak tree is 100 to
300 years. This particular oak might live until 2119 to 2319.
This is the average life span. They actually may live up to
1000 years.

In 2024 that acorn finally grew and became this little tree
of 24 cm high. Butler's novel starts on 20 July 2024. I am
now 38 years old in 2024. Butler would have been 77 years
old. Lauren Oya Olamina is just 15 years old.

"Then we buried our dead and we planted oak trees. After-
ward, we sat together and talked and ate a meal and decided
to call this place Acorn."

I almost threw away this little oak sapling twice because I
thought it was dead. Once it lost all its leaves and once my
cat ate them all. Luckily I didn't. I hope to plant it in a piece
of land one day. It's a time capsule of hope.

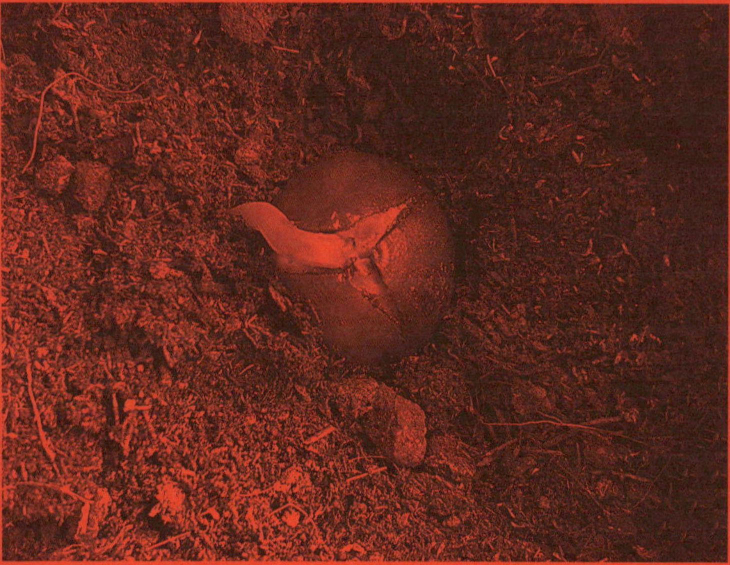

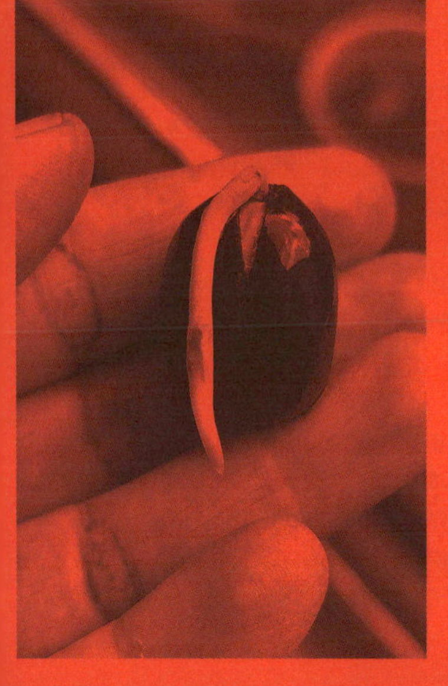

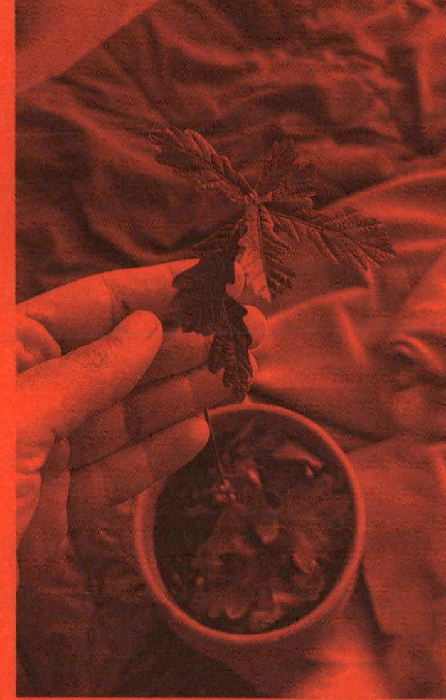

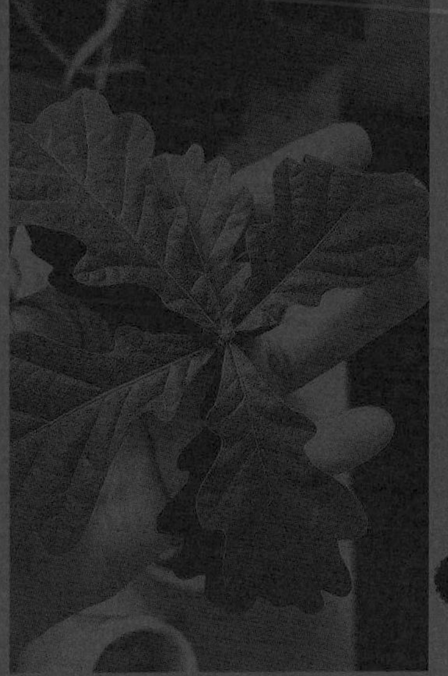

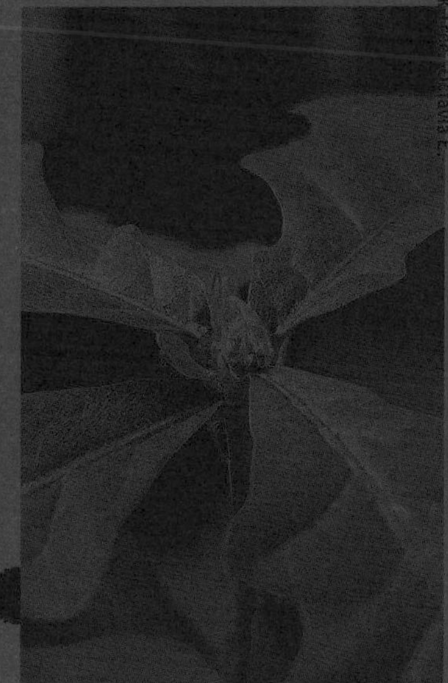

Müge Yılmaz – Acorn / An Oak Tree / Octavia E.

ANCESTRAL LINDEN LEMONADE
BY MARJOLEIN VAN DER LOO

Linden trees are very popular in urban spaces; they are quite easy to maintain and have a majestic appearance.[1] The scent of their blossoms at the start of summer is wonderful. Many cities choose Linden lanes and even proudly use them for city marketing. For centuries, the trees played an important role and are known for their feminine energy, as a refuge, a place of oath, and holy for the Celts and Germanics. Yet, Linden trees used to be common in forests. In the Netherlands, there are only two old-growth forests left where one can find old Linden trees, they are located close to each other: Savelsbos and Vijlenerbos, both a stone's throw from Maastricht.

The decline of the Linden forest is coherent with the onset of agriculture, the start of what we call the Neolithic, and where, some argue, the Anthropocene started. The first settlers, living in small groups and attending a modest farm, cut down the number of Lindens drastically. They (probably) loved the wood for its softness and as herbage to feed their kettle. By cutting many of the large trees, they created open spaces in the dense forests, which attracted Hazel, an invaluable staple for a mixed agricultural and foraging lifestyle. The knowledge, sensitivity, and ability of these people migrating from the Southeast of Europe to read the landscape and

---

1   Linden trees from the genus *Tilia* are in English speaking countries also known as Lime Trees.

manage it were incredible. Western science is slowly catching up with their insights into the characteristics of the environments they chose for their dwellings about 7.000 years ago.

Rediscovering the joy of gathering blossoms, leaves, fruits, and nuts, once erased from many capitalist cultures, can be a thrilling adventure. By labeling it as a poor people's activity and dangerous for one's health, many have forgotten the whats and hows.[2] However, foraging allows a closer connection to the vibrant plant life in our (urban) environment. It's a journey of personal and intimate relations, of observing the changes through seasons and years. It heightens our senses, making our nearby streets, parks, and forests a treasure trove of flavors and aromas.

Indigenous botanist Robin Wall Kimmerer formulates a guideline for foraging through what she calls 'the honorable harvest.'[3] This method starts from a relationship of reciprocity that acknowledges the gift of the plant and makes space for a contribution and responsibility by the gatherer. Similarly significant is observing the quantity of what you want to gather. This method allows only foraging in cases of abundance. However, in any situation, you only take what you need for your purpose.

Before cutting or picking, you observe the plant and introduce yourself and your intentions. Then, you ask for permission as a way to acknowledge you are not on a one way street. Further, it practically suggests cutting with a clean sharp tool to limit damage. If available, a woven basket is ideal as it allows critters to crawl out of your crop. Another important tip for foraging is

---

2   Alexis Nikole, known as @Blackforager, made insightful videos on the cultural politics behind class and race history and foraging. Check the post on Feb 13, 2024.

3   Read more in Robin Wall Kimmerer, *Braiding Sweetgrass*, 2013.

the location and height. You need to consider the fumes and pollution in a city that is often increased nearby roads. Check the infrastructure and consider the health of the plant before selecting and picking. In regards to rabies, it's recommendable to collect only above knee height. Needless to say, always rinse your findings before consuming.

Walks are also great for observing trees and looking at their processes, flowers, and fruits. This can be a process done over many walks and cycling routes in which you establish your favorite vegetal partners for foraging. Many handbooks and smartphone applications are helpful in determining species, but you could also ask a friend or another human who is around.

By the start of June, the sweet floral smell of Linden blossoms can be found on many city streets in Europe and on the East coast of Turtle Island.[4] So why not enjoy them more than monumental urban green? Return to the practice of foraging, as largely practiced by ancestors, while enjoying the flavors reminiscent of the old-growth forests. Treat your body with the memories and stories of the land and the ones who came before us with a self-picked Linden tea or homemade Linden Cordial.

You can pick and dry the flowers and use them as a tisane infusion all year round. Their anti-inflammatory properties work amazingly against colds and coughs. Moreover, the blossoms act as relaxants and have been used to treat anxiety. Besides, when the summer kicks in, it's an even nicer treat when you have syrup to drink with sparkling water or to add to desserts.

---

4 A name for North America used by some indigenous people.

LIME BLOSSOM CORDIAL

INGREDIENTS
3 hands full of lime blossoms
500 ml organic apple juice
200 gr sugar
1 organic lemon

SUPPLIES
strainer
glass bottle
kitchen towel or cheesecloth
pot with lid

1. Spread your blossoms on a towel, check and remove critters, then put the flowers in your pot
2. Bring the apple juice to a boil and pour over the blossoms
3. Cut the organic lemon into four parts, remove the seeds, and add
4. Close the pot with a lid and drape a blanket or towel around the pot to hold its remaining warmth and leave for about 24hrs
5. Strain the mixture by using the cheesecloth in the strainer; this might take a while when there's a lot of residue
6. Prepare the glass bottle by disinfecting it with boiling water
7. Heat and dissolve the sugar in the sifted liquid and cook for one minute
8. Pour the cordial into the warm bottle; close it, and let it cool

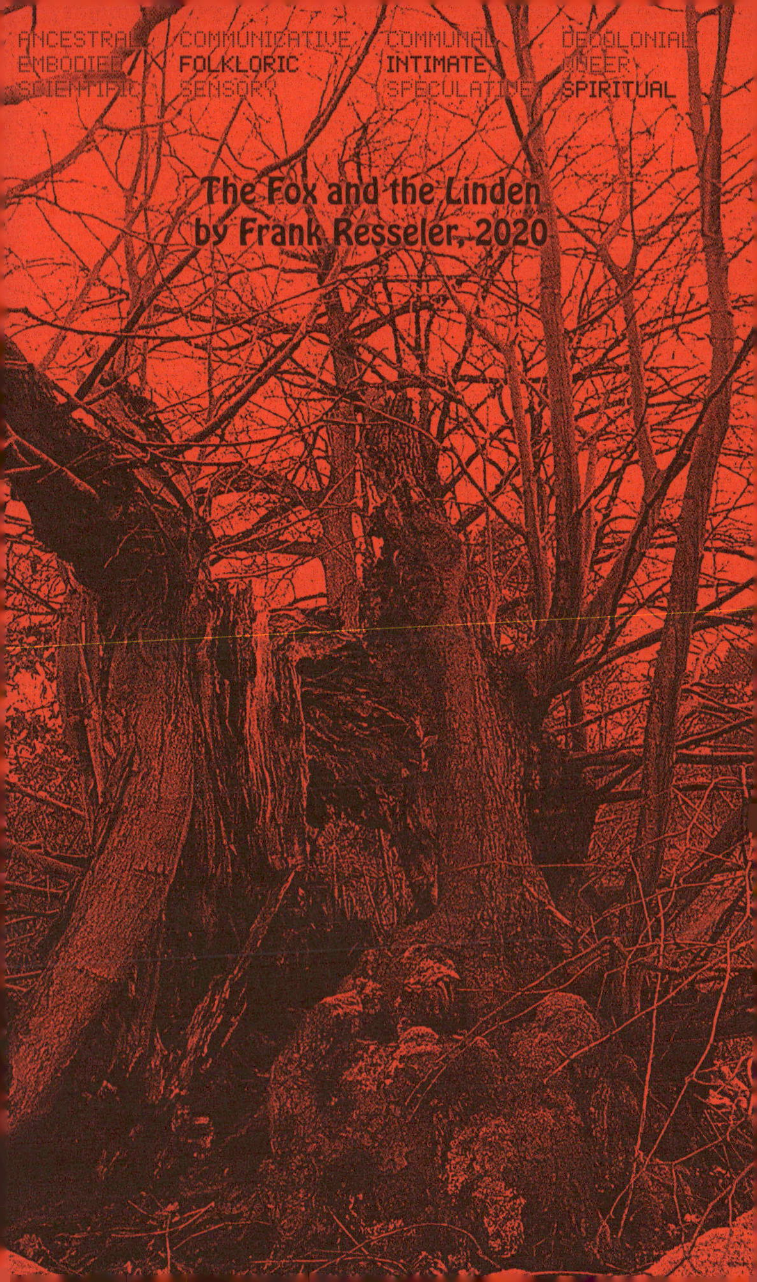
ANCESTRAL   COMMUNICATIVE   COMMUNAL   DECOLONIAL
EMBODIED / IN   FOLKLORIC   INTIMATE   QUEER
SCIENTIFIC   SENSORY   SPECULATIVE   SPIRITUAL

The Fox and the Linden
by Frank Resseler, 2020

ANCESTRAL   COMMUNICATIVE   COMMUNAL   DECOLONIAL
EMBODIED   FOLKLORIC   INTIMATE   QUEER
SCIENTIFIC   SENSORY   SPECULATIVE   SPIRITUAL

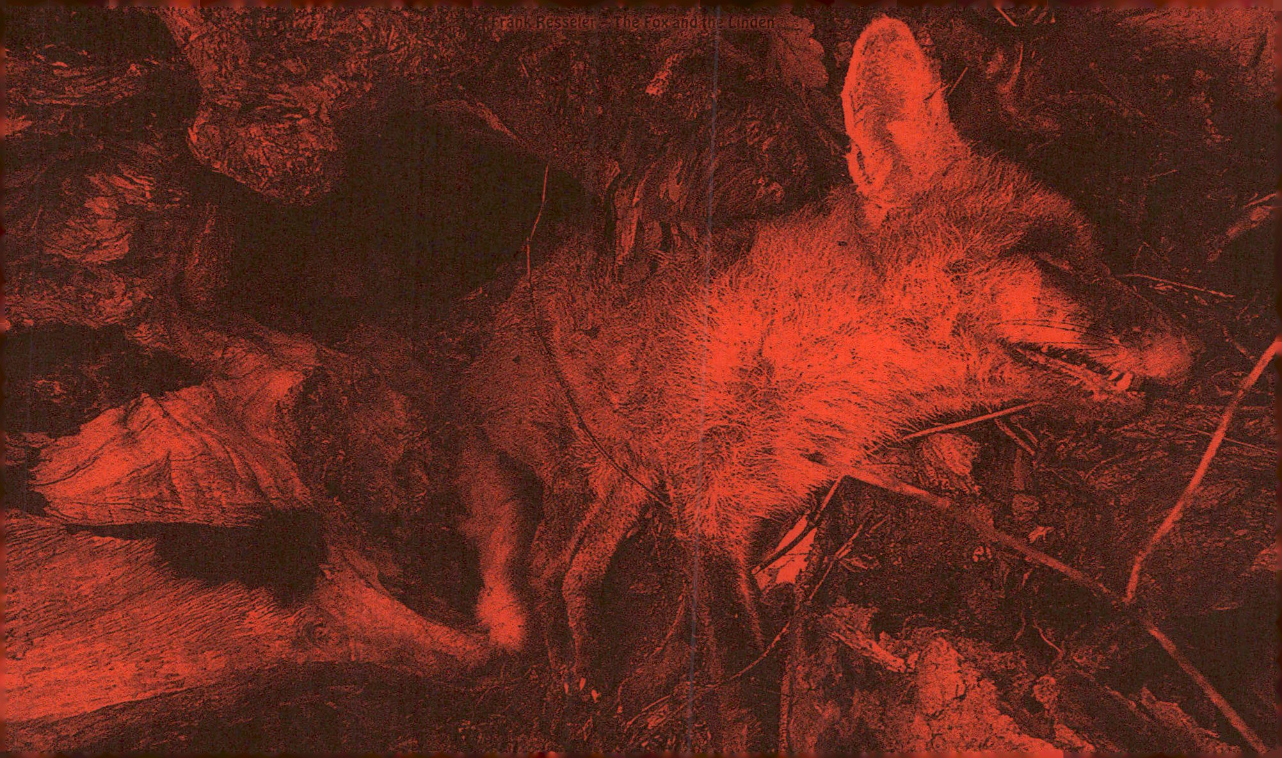
Frank Resseler – The Fox and the Linden

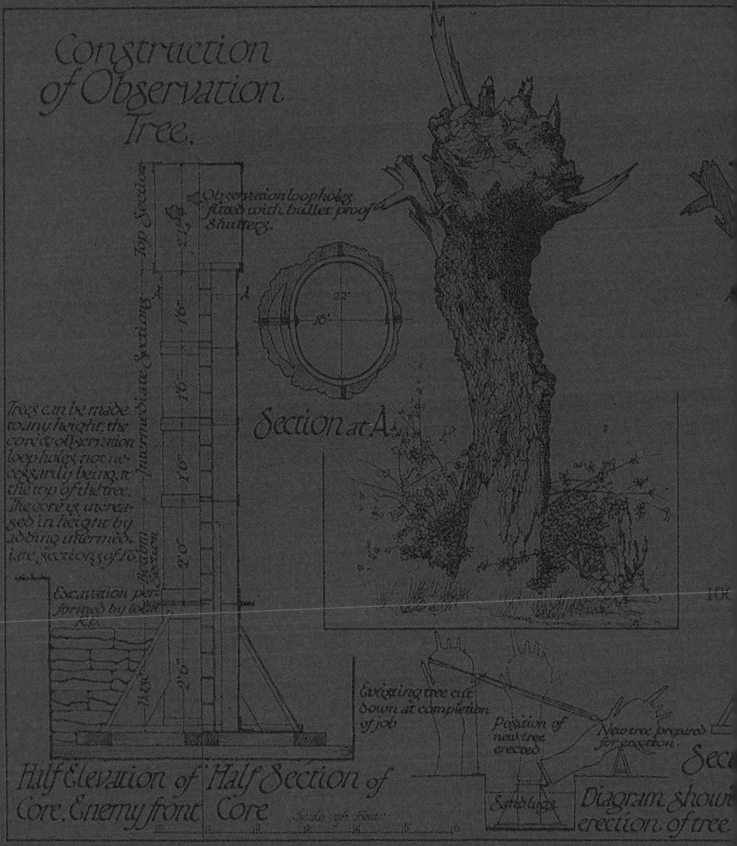

Construction of Observation Tree.

Top Section

Intermediate Sections

Bottom Section

Observation loop holes fitted with bullet proof shutters.

22"

16"

Section at A.

Trees can be made to any height, the core & observation loop holes not necessarily being at the top of the tree. The core is increased in height by adding intermeds. i.e. sections of 10'.

Excavation performed by R.E.

2'6"   1'6"   1'6"   2'0"   2'0"   2'6"

Existing tree cut down at completion of job

Position of new tree erected

New tree prepared for erection

Sandbags

Half Elevation of Core, Enemy front | Half Section of Core

Scale of Feet

Section

Diagram showing erection of tree

(34)

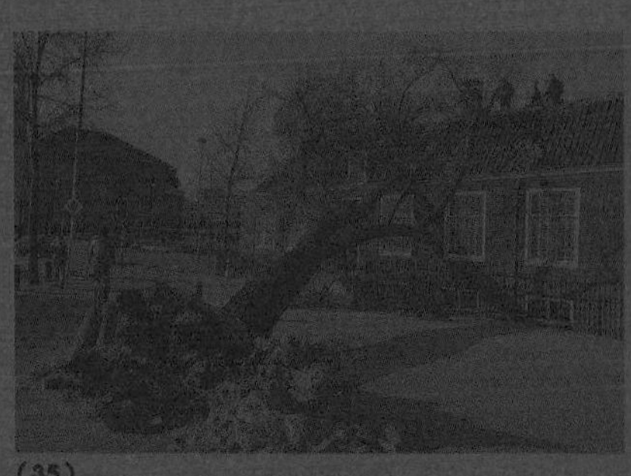

(35)

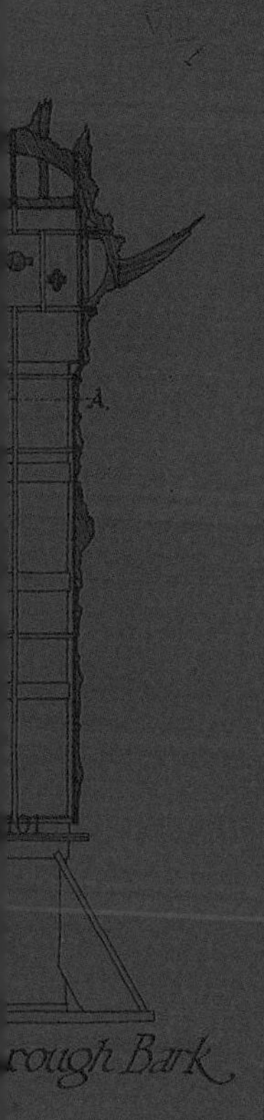

rough Bark 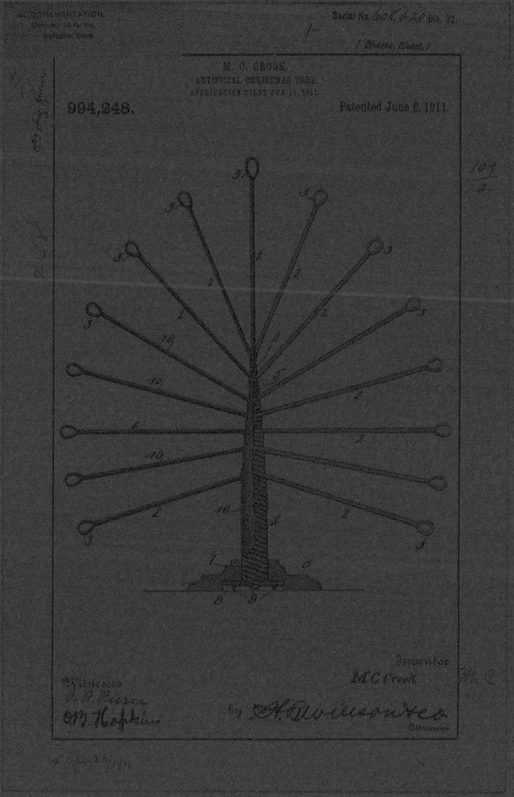
A.

ORNAMENTATION.
Ornamental for the
Imitation trees.
Serial No. 608,420 Div. 32.
1 Sheets, Sheet 1.
M. C. CROOK.
ARTIFICIAL CHRISTMAS TREE.
APPLICATION FILED FEB. 13, 1911.
994,248.
Patented June 6, 1911
Witnesses
J. R. Pierce
O. B. Hopkins
Inventor
M. C. Crook
by
Attorney

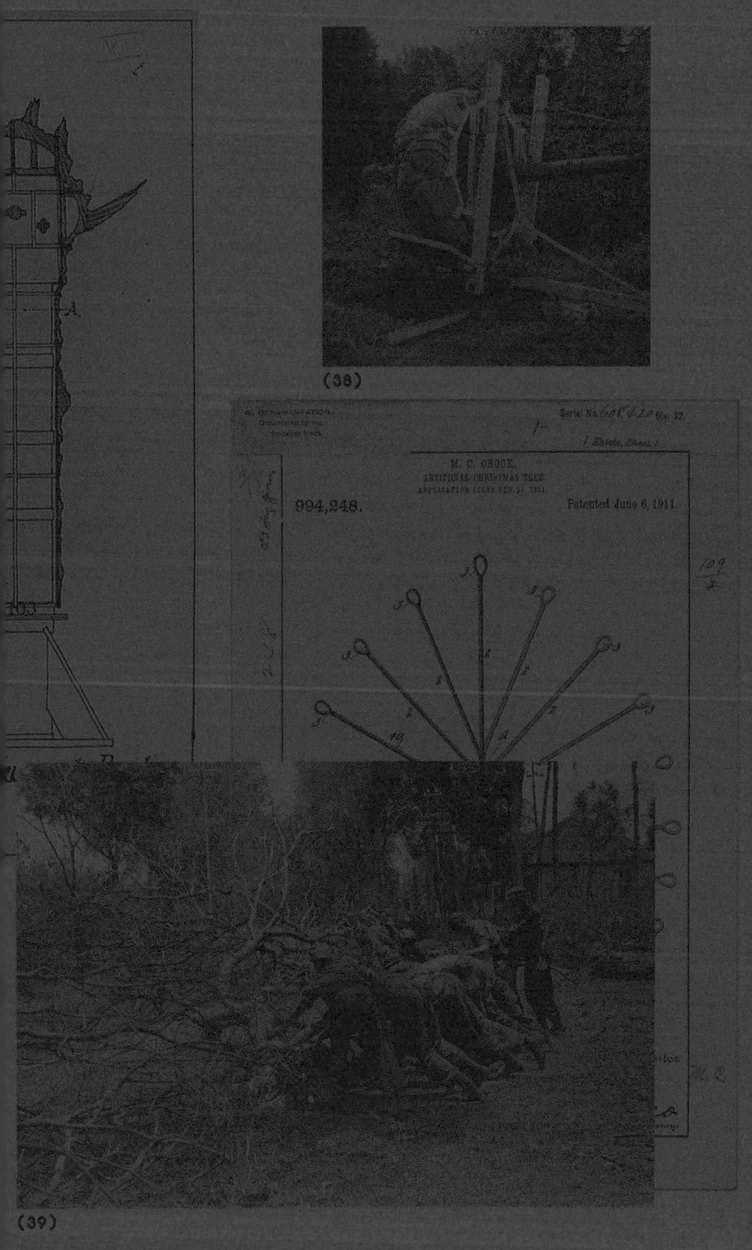

(38)
81. ORNAMENTATION.
Ornamental forms.
Imitation trees.
Serial No. 608,420 Div. 32.
1 Sheets, Sheet 1.
M. C. GROSS.
ARTIFICIAL CHRISTMAS TREE.
APPLICATION FILED FEB. 15, 1911.
994,248.
Patented June 6, 1911.
(39)

Construction
of Observation
II
pag. 211.   Vol. 1.   L. 2.
Intermediate Sections — Top Section
Trees can be made
to any height, the
core of observation
loopholes not ne-
cessarily being at
the top of the tree.
The core is increas-
ed in height by
adding intermed-
iate sections of 16 ft
Excavation per-
formed by ...
RE.
Half El...
Core, &...
New tree prepared
for erection.
104
Hulett Sculp
(40)

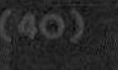

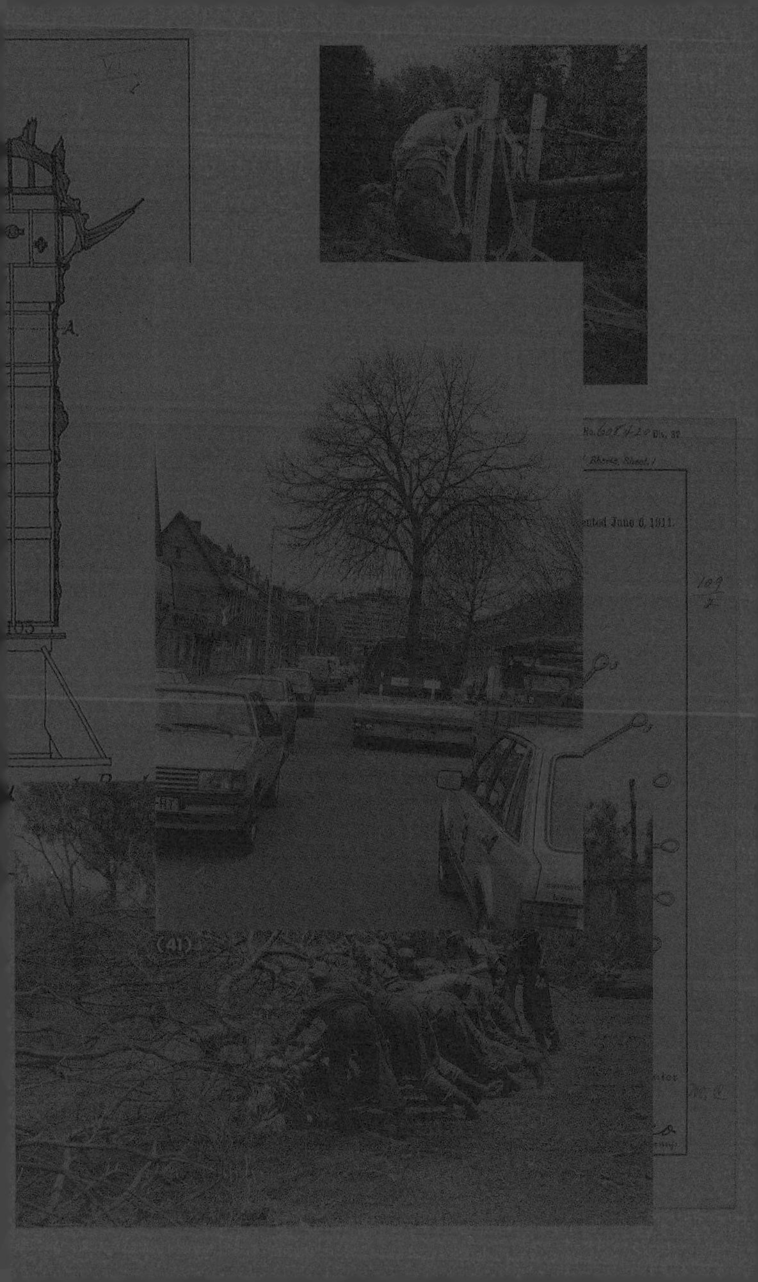

Construction of Observation Tr

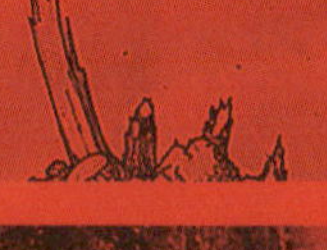

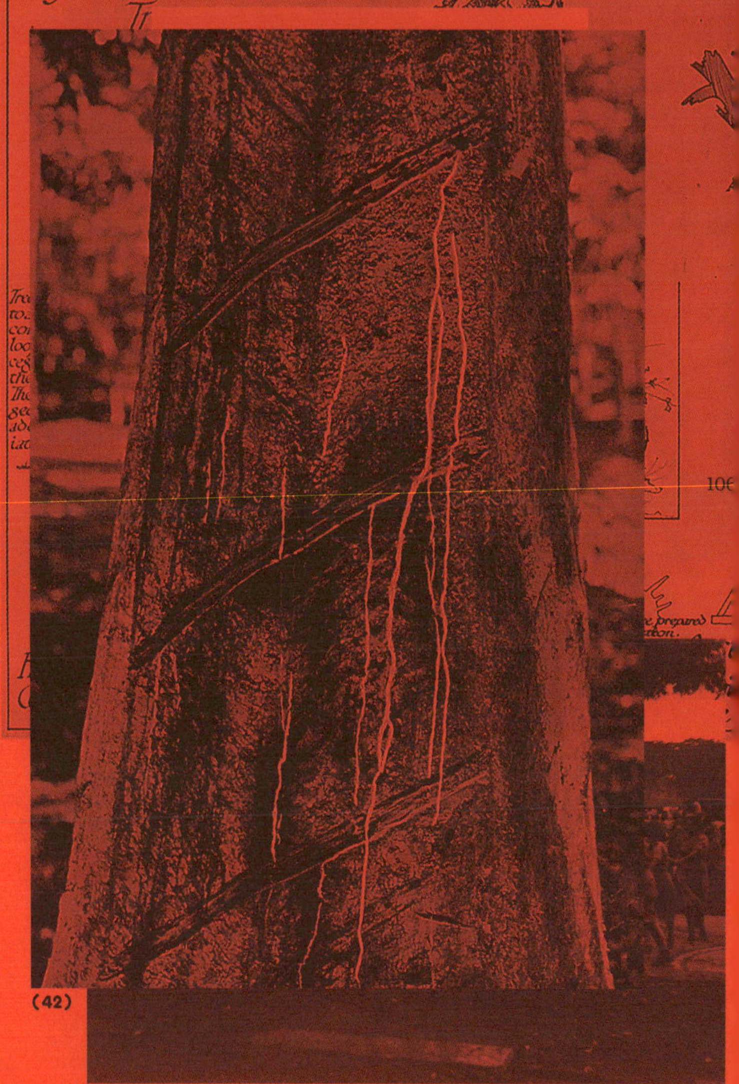

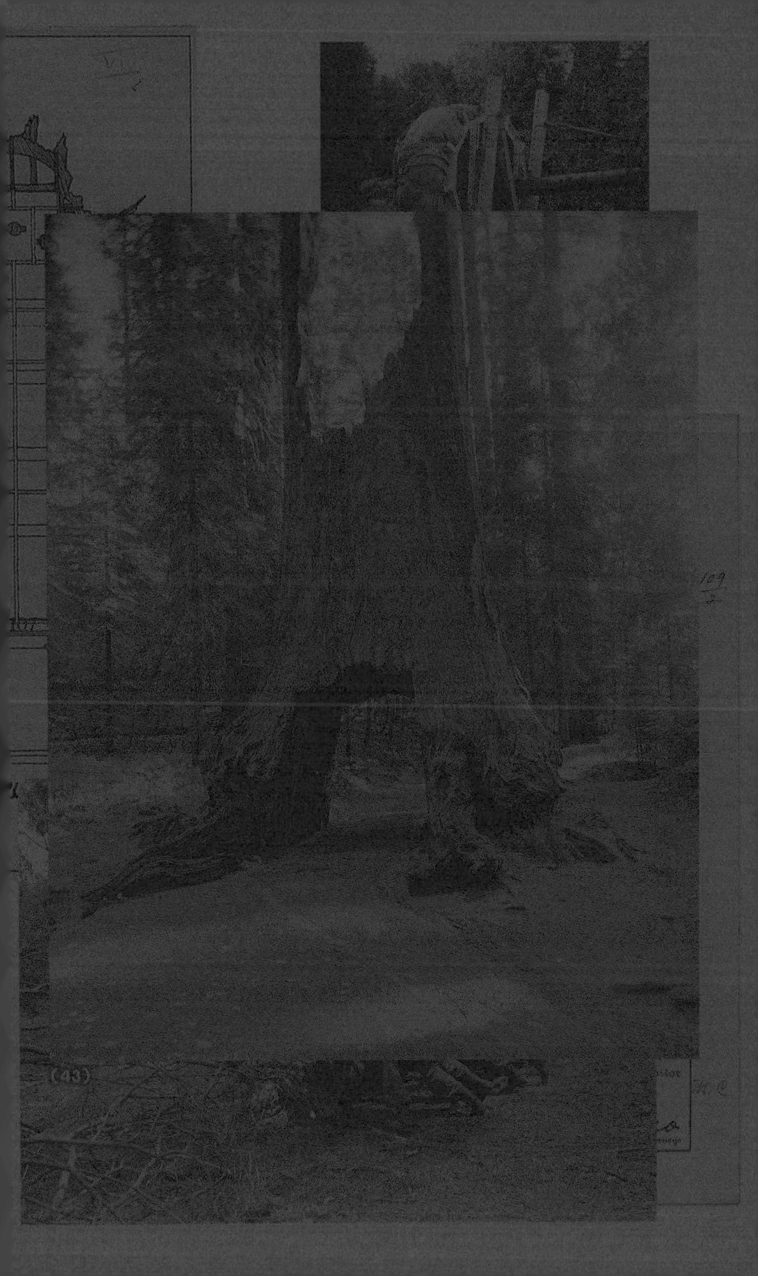

ON A TRAJECTORY THROUGH A MAZE OF TRAJECTORIES

SCULPTURE FROM LOCALLY HARVESTED PINE WOOD

BY GERBRAND BURGER, 2024

This work was made on the occasion of the launch of the Thinking Forest Foundation at Landgoed Welna, where the foundation presents a program of events for 2024 and 2025. Thinking Forest is an initiative by artist Gerbrand Burger. It's a radically sustainable exhibition space where ecology, contemporary art, and science meet in a production forest. The double meaning of 'thinking forest' points to both the natural wisdom of the forest as an ecosystem and a place to think, reflect, and learn; an organic model for the development and the spreading of seedling ideas. Within the forest, art and wood production, decay, biodiversity, science, and a public program come together. Thus, the notion of a 'production forest' can be reimagined as beneficial to all of the living world and to heal human partnership with the land.

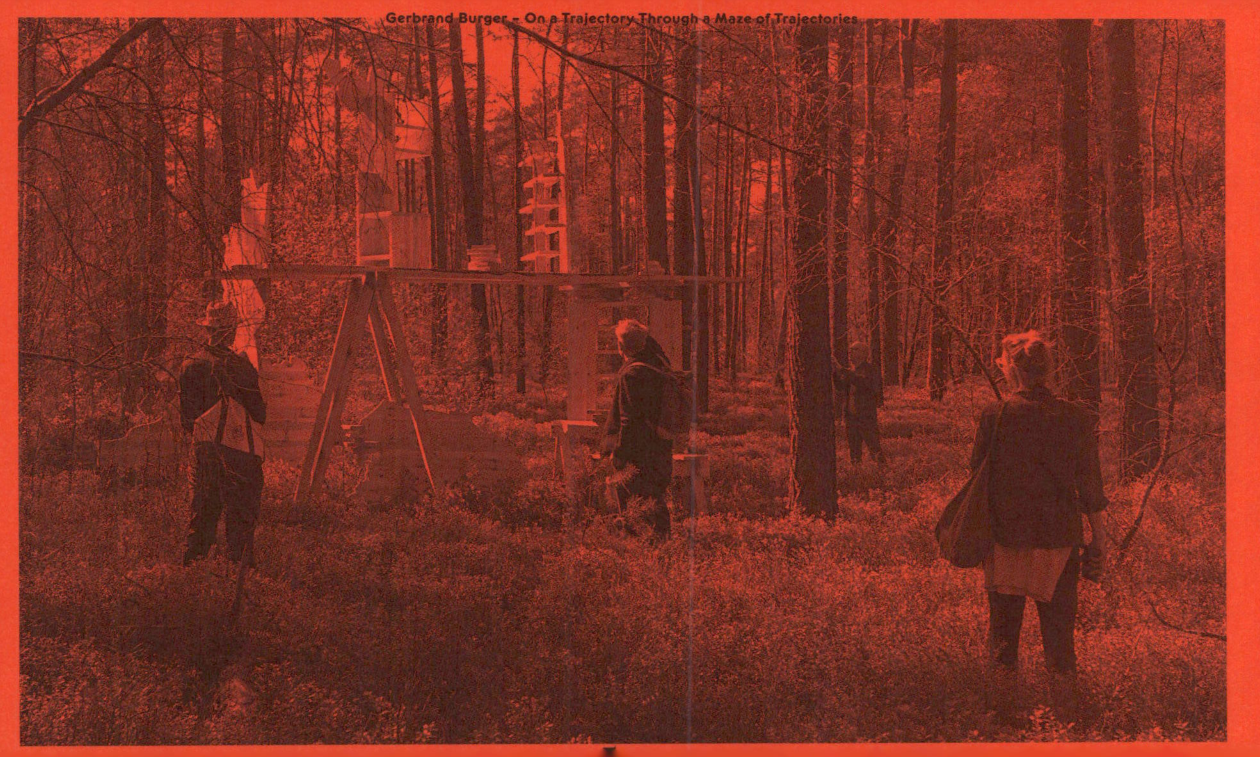

Gerbrand Burger – On a Trajectory Through a Maze of Trajectories

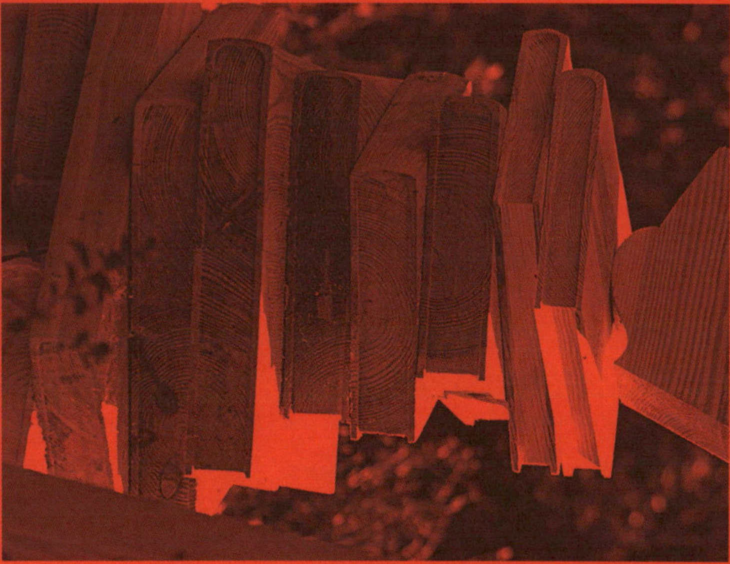

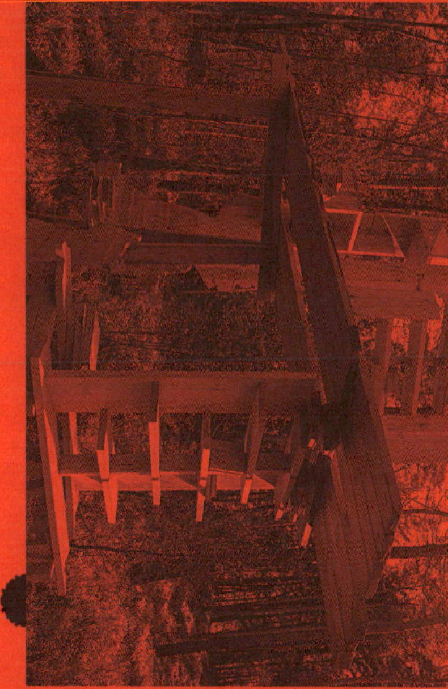

20-07-2018
by Jerrold Saija

After spending a week on the main island of Ambon, we
took the boat to the east neighboring island of Haruku.
Like the many other neighboring islands, Haruku's lush
forest and nature contrast the bustling city landscape of
Ambon. On the southeast shore is a town called Aboru.
This is where my ancestral lineages on both sides of my
family are rooted.

    After a few days in Aboru, my grandfather and I sponta-
neously accompanied my uncle to the jungle. The three
of us took the shuttle bus from Aboru inwards, moving from
an open area to densely grown roads of trees towering
meters above us. We drove uphill, downhill, and through
many bends and curves on the road; after half an hour,
my uncle signaled the driver to stop, and we got off the bus
in the middle of nowhere. The asphalt road behind us
looks as familiar as the road in front of us. We followed the
road in front for a bit. I listened to the flapping sandals
of my grandfather and I followed the steps of my uncle's
rain boots. The sound of two unprepared people going
into the jungle.

My uncle guided us into the jungle and knew where to get
off the road and into the woods. We left the asphalt road
and were immersed in the abundance of the forest. Prepared with his machete, he cleared the path deeper into
the woods. The colorful insects crawling along the forest
floor didn't scare me; instead, I felt curious and perceptive
as I followed my uncle and grandfather deeper into the
forest. My sense of time was lost, my eyes focused, and I

could breathe deeply. The spirit of the forest seemed to embrace us, welcoming us into its midst. Its essence is deeply connected to my Moluccan heritage, and I felt like I was exactly where I was meant to be.

While we followed my uncle, he pronounced our location with a distinctive whistling noise. Another whistle echoed back from somewhere deeper in the jungle. They signaled each other with whistling, and we followed the sound back and forth. I felt a bit disoriented but not lost, as I felt one with the land. Time passed unnoticed as we walked until we reached our destination. Deep in the jungle, we found a group of four men collectively working together, cutting and processing a big Sagu tree.

This was my first time seeing the concept of 'masohi' first-hand. Masohi, meaning mutual cooperation, is a cultural practice that is common among the people of the Moluccas. Working together as a collective has been a traditional practice in the Moluccas, passed down through genera-tions. It has become an essential aspect of Moluccan heritage and identity, and it still plays an important role in Moluccas' daily life. Becoming acquainted with the jungle was a profound experience; it was the only place where seeing masohi in this specific context made sense. The journey into the woods was so vivid and immersive that I can't recall exactly how we returned. I was completely absorbed, and for the first time, I felt a connection to the 'lands'. Touching the bark of a massive Sagu tree up close was incredible, yet it was also the moment when the tree was felled. This intense experience of working together and feeling connected added to the depth of the moment.

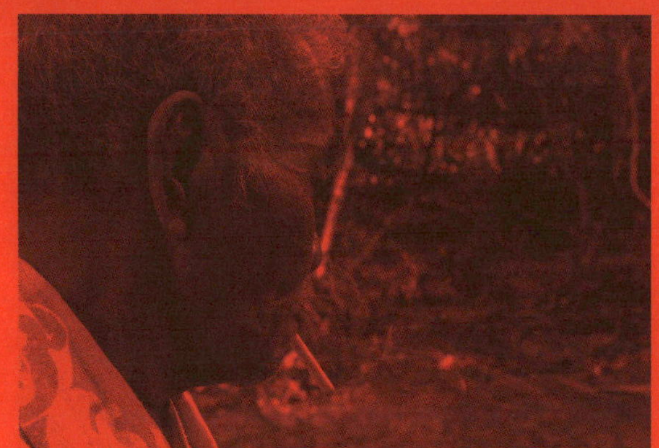

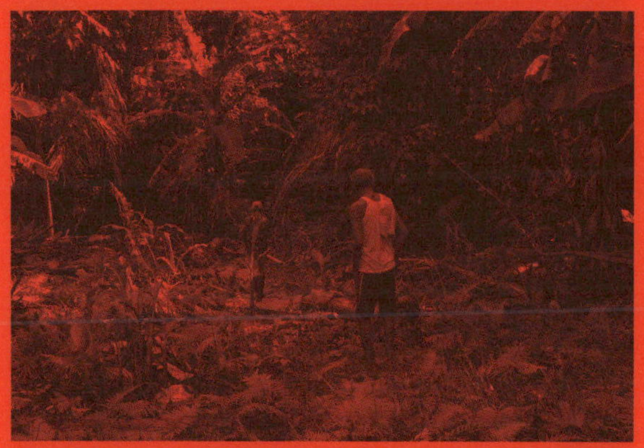

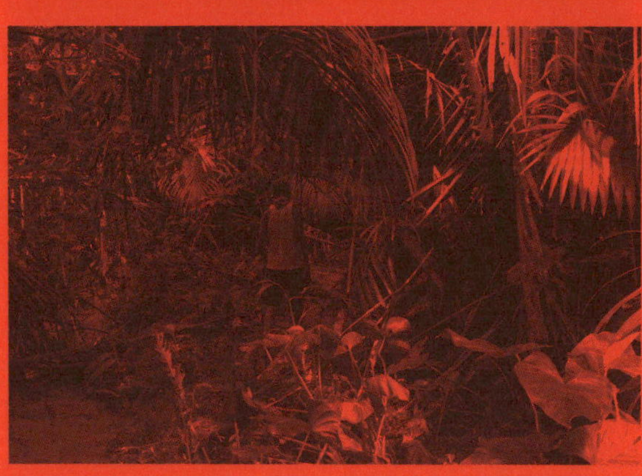

Jerrold Saija – 20-07-2018

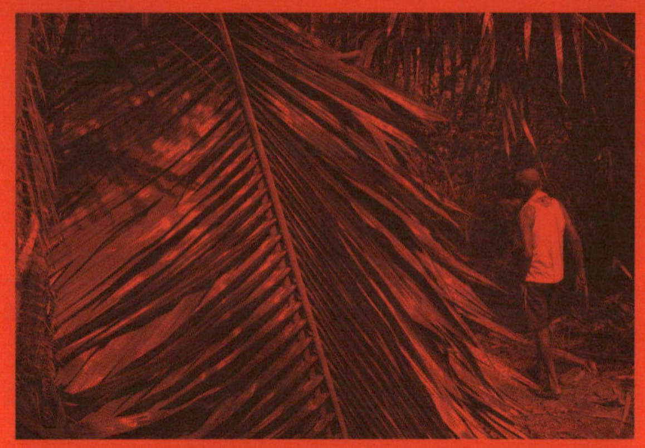

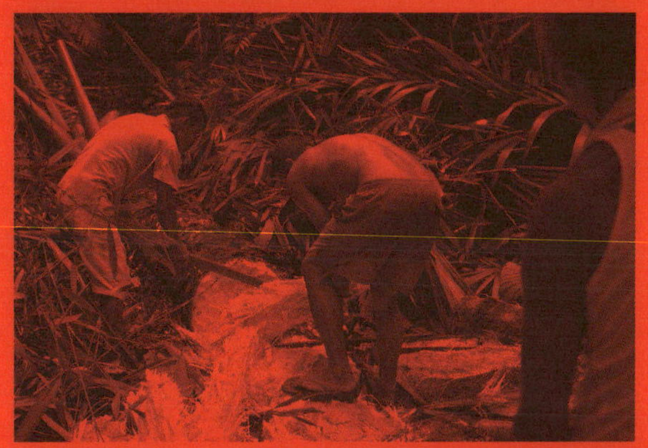

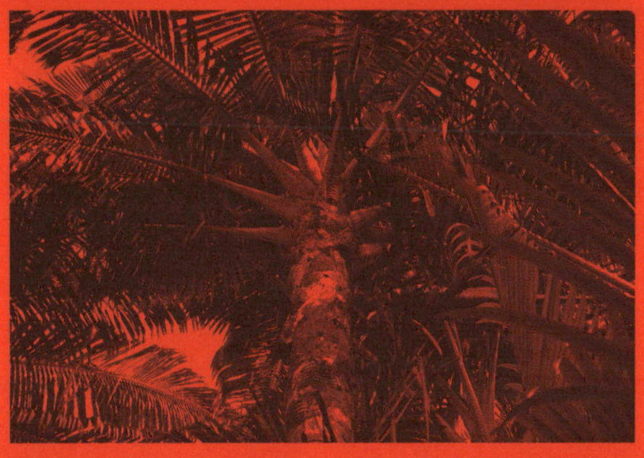

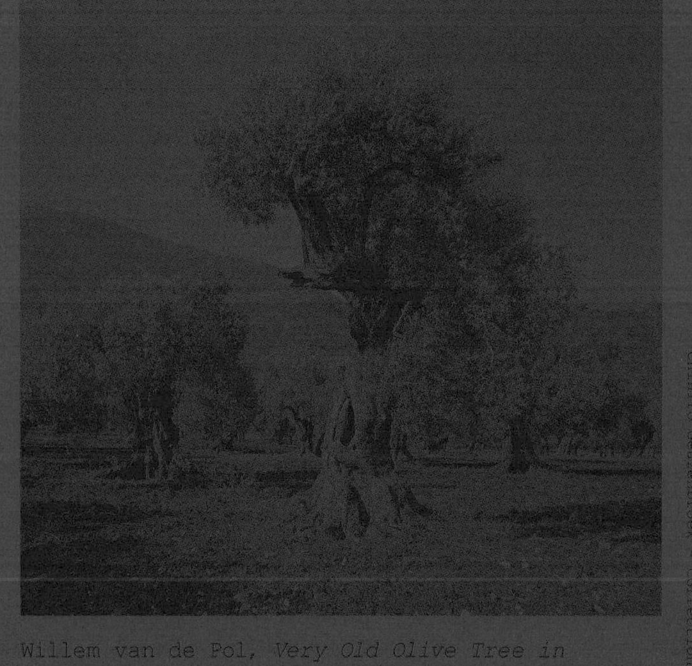

15

Willem van de Pol, *Very Old Olive Tree in Orchard in Israel*, 1964   (Photo: Nationaal Archief, CC0)

Correction: Very old Palestinian heritage
              appropriated by Israeli land grabbing.
Correction: Stolen sisters before their family
              gets uprooted in their millions.
Correction: Indigenous friends targeted by the
              Israeli military for their sumud.*
Correction: A call to action to defend the sacred!
              The original *seed keepers* who never
              forget… how to plant again.

*sumud = steadfastness/perseverance

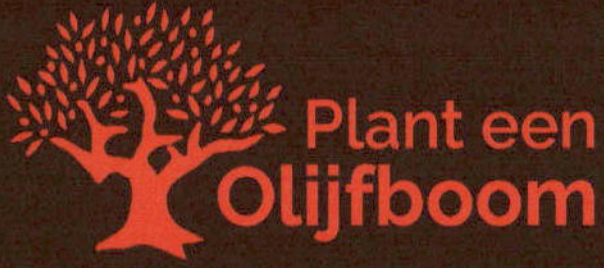

Sponsorship Certificate

Plant een Olijfboom (Plant an Olive Tree) pledges to plant an olive tree in Palestine in the name of

Onomatopee

This tree supports Palestinian farmers in their struggle to keep their land and to keep hope alive for a just peace with equality for all citizens.

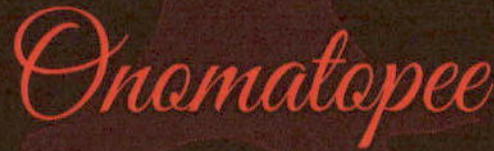

PRIMORDIAL TONGUES OR THE
LANGUAGE OF NON-AUTONOMOUS BEINGS
BY KAREN LOFGREN

I love to imagine that we can speak to trees in a common cellular primordial language, and I like to think that trees can remember when we were worms. Before the split, a couple billion years ago, we were all the same type of single celled organism. As we all developed collars, and nobody knows why we did this, we began to consume other single celled organisms, then we split into groups which are annoyingly called "kingdoms", but nobody knows really why we split. I'm sort of guessing that was a numbers game.

Is there anything in us, in our cells, that bears "memory" of this period? Is there a way to access a type of consciousness that can openly converse with the plant "kingdom" in the language of our shared past? Gardeners and psychonauts would say yes. As much of our DNA remains similar to our remote ancestors, it would make sense that real communication is possible. What is the basis of this language and how do we access communication with plant beings? If we meditate or consume 'teacher' plants, can we get to a place of cellular memory, can we remember when we, as cells, all had collars?

Can we talk to trees through our bacteria and fungi as trees speak to each other and share resources through a similar network of organisms? Alkaloid containing

Fear Extinction, 2023   Cast bronze, cast orgonite with metals and medicinal plants: datura flowers, white sage, wormwood
148 cm × 66 cm × 10 cm

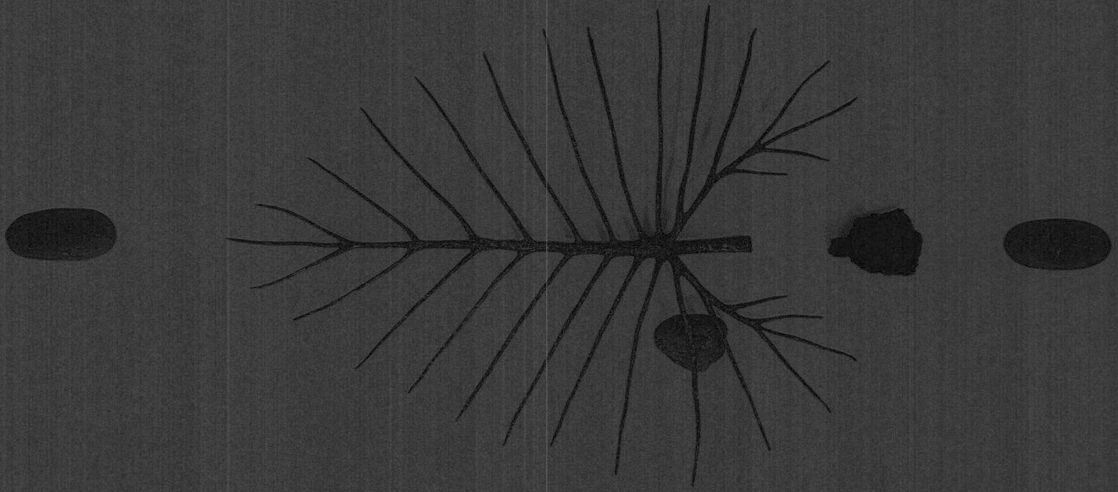

plants evolved with us, and we have used those plants to alter our perception of space and time, or have they used us? To learn plant language, or is it poison? Some say these alkaloids developed in plants as defense mechanisms, chemical warfare against attackers. Others say that the plants want to speak to us in the language of their spirits, which coevolved with us in dialogue to fuck with our consciousness and adapt to their needs. To become their allies and protectors.

I like to imagine "autonomous" bodies, plant bodies and animal bodies, including human bodies, as not one type of any thing, but as communities of organisms, speaking with other multiplicities of organisms which we identify as "beings" or "things". I like to picture the language we use as images, and then to use those images to help to shape what work I can make. The familiarity of the visual language used in some sculptures, paintings, seems to speak to that collared cell, tugs at something we know but we haven't seen before. To me, this is the language of art, that it can speak to something older and simpler than humans, or more complex. Conifers have seven times the amount of DNA than we do, and a Japanese Canopy plant has 50 times the amount of DNA as us. I sometimes wonder if they think of us, and if they do, if they consider us still worms. Worms can colonize and devastate probably as well as we can. I like to think they see us that way.

Joss Allen
Colonsay

We left the bikes under lind
sticky with flourish
propped against
stone and dyke
We heaved over
heading northeast up muddling track
soon dry heathered rock

We did not yet know of trysting-tree
or wallwood A' Choille Mhòr
hearts sought wud
sought ancient boughs
to rest young limbs
embrace

Clambered
steel wire
larch posts
steep bank
bracken
to gurly trees
Up to holt and hag-wood

to face oaken kink
bole and browl
we climbed
awe stricken
and green
we climbed to claff
along leomen we grinned

Limbs and lips and fingers
holding dear
we traced
the shape of leaves
against sky
and called out to vitality
beneath lichenskin

Later, we stripped our bark bare
and laid smoothed white-legs
buttocks
shank
on being and hope

Sea cooled, we set off hame-o'er
salty
ozoned
in love
arboreal.

Glossary

A' Choille Mhòr .... placename, 'great wood'
being .... beach of seashore
browl .... small branches
claff .... where the trunk of a tree
.... splits into branches
dyke .... wall
flourish .... blossom
gurly .... gnarled, rough
hag-wood .... small group of trees,
.... coppiced perhaps?
hame-o'er .... homeward
heathered .... covered in heather
holt .... wooded hill
hope .... cove, inlet
leomen .... branch, bough
lichenskin .... covered in lichen
lind .... linden tree
muddling .... muddy, ineffective path
ozoned .... spray from the sea
shank .... trunk of tree, or human
trysting-tree .... tree where lovers might meet
wall-wood .... wild wood
wud .... wood, substance of trees

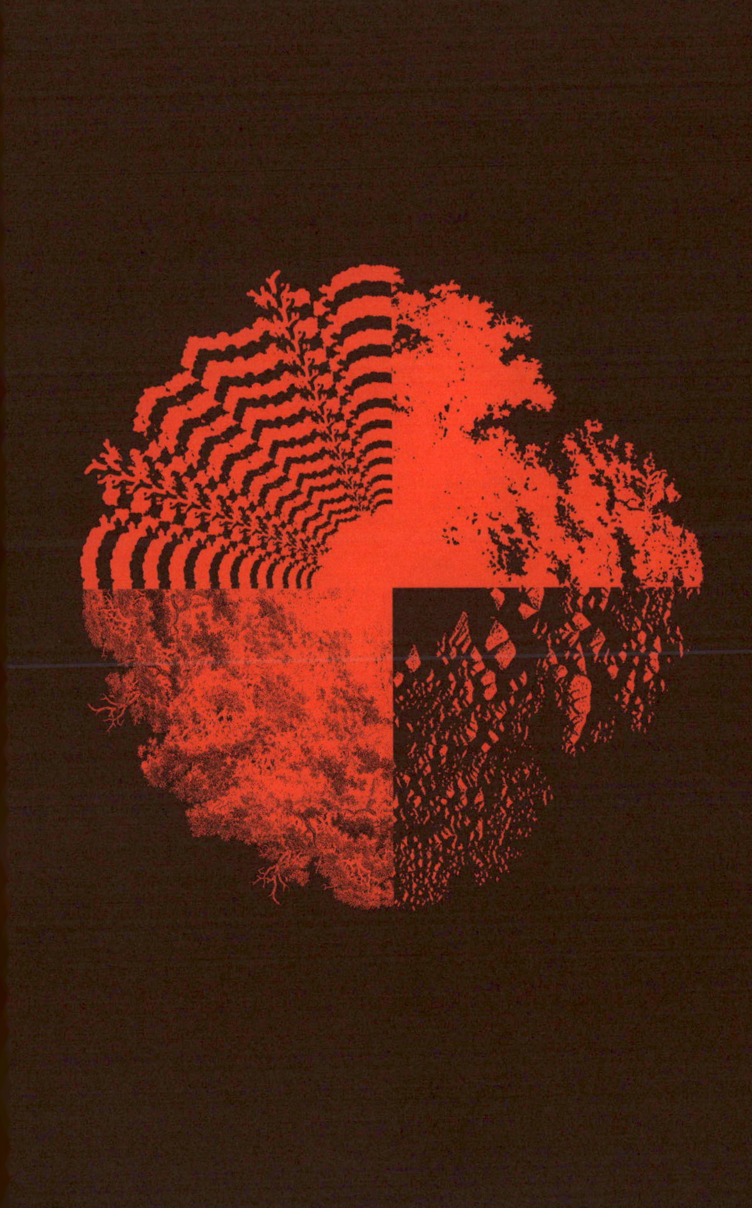

JOSS ALLEN

Joss Allen is an artworker and researcher; he / they can be found in the garden, amongst the weeds and compost heaps.

....

CÉLINE BAUMANN

Céline Baumann is a French landscape architect, through an intersectional lens she aims to create dynamic open spaces informed by the interactive ecology between people and nature.

....

BÁRBARA SÁNCHEZ BARROSO

Bárbara Sánchez Barroso is an artist who likes to read, write, shoot analog films, and take long walks in the city, daydreaming about being in the countryside.

....

JORGE MENNA BARRETO

Jorge Menna Barreto is a Brazilian artist and educator who teaches at UC Santa Cruz and is interested in agroforestry, land art, site-specificity, plant-based food, and multispecies assemblages.

....

GERBRAND BURGER

Gerbrand Burger is a visual artist who makes sculptures and site-specific interventions embedding art in natural processes inspired by his practice of sustainable forestry.

....

RENÉE BUS

Renée Bus is an artist who creates a symbiosis between humans and the non-human world through sculpture, performance and language exploring of life, death, time, and place.

....

LUCY DAVIS

Lucy Davis is a visual artist, art writer, and founder of The Migrant Ecologies Projects, whose transdisciplinary practice encircles plant genetics, tree lore, and bird song as well as art/science, naturecultures, memory, materiality, narrative environments, and most recently, pyscho-ecologies of resilience.

....

AMIRIO FREEMAN

Amirio Freeman is a writer, interviewer, and Scorpio exploring the relationship between humans and our beyond-human kin through a Black, queer lens.

....

CHIHIRO GEUZENBROEK

Chihiro Geuzenbroek is a Bolivian- Dutch multidisciplinary artist, writer, organizer, trainer in decolonial climate justice perspectives and practices.

....

FEMKE HABETS

Femke Habets is a contemporary artist who draws the whispers of stones she encounters and cherishes a cup of tea that shimmers with the metallic colors of rainbows.

RODERICK HIETBRINK

Roderick Hietbrink is a contemporary Dutch visual artist living and working in Oslo.

INGELA IHRMAN

In her artistic practice, Ingela Ihrman observes how we humans simultaneously romanticize and exploit nature, even though we are part of it and depend on it.

MANJOT KAUR

Manjot Kaur is a contemporary Indian artist who works with drawings, paintings, and time-based media in an attempt to de-patriarchate the sovereignty of ecology and women's bodies.

MARI KESKI-KORSU

Mari Keski-Korsu is a post-disciplinary researcher and artist who explores micro-level manifestations of the ecological poly-crisis, whose work is based on multi-species collaborations, expressed through a hybrid combination of participatory performance, visual, and live art.

ALICE LADENBURG

The artistic practice of Alice Ladenburg combines autoethnographic research with scientific methods to promote a deeper and more nuanced understanding of our planet during a period of environmental crisis.

MARJOLEIN VAN DER LOO

Marjolein van der Loo is a multidisciplinary researcher with a passion for ecologies and a social agenda whose practice ranges between curatorial, artistic, editorial, and pedagogical work.

KAREN LOFGREN

Karen Lofgren is a Los Angeles-based Canadian visual artist whose feminist and decolonial research centers on the living world: ritual, history, medicine, and how our cultural systems connect to other wild systems. She is a Guggenheim Fellow, a Pollock Krasner grantee, and a Fulbright Core Scholar.

HIRA NABI

Hira Nabi is an artist whose practice is concerned with meditations on the environment, the often unseen, and a slow process of re-earthing: by which she intends to shift focus away from anthropocentric stories into a more interconnected, and larger witnessing of the times we live in.

YANNICK NUSS

Studio Yannick Nuss is a graphic design studio focusing on the creation of books, visual identities and exhibitions, working in cooperation with artists, cultural institutions and universities, with the intention to create contemporary and relevant printed matter.

FRANK RESSELER

Frank Resseler is a biologist, documentary maker, and storyteller sharing his fascination with the local environments of Nationaal Park Hoge Kempen and the ecology of the river Meuse border region between Belgium and the Netherlands.

ANNE RICHTER

Anne Richter is a Belgian author, editor and scholar, who in addition to her own fiction, is known for editing an international anthology of female fantastical writers, essays about women writers and fantastical literature.

JERROLD SAIJA

Jerrold Saija is a visual artist who focuses on colonization and decolonization and the deep marks this has left on Moluccan society in general and the Moluccan body in particular.

OSCAR SALGUERO

Oscar Salguero is an archivist, book curator, independent researcher, and initiator of Interspecies Library.

Interspecies Library is the first archive dedicated to the curation and advancement of artists' books focused on alternative interspecies futures. Email *info@interspecieslibrary.com* to plan a visit to the library in Brooklyn, New York.

SANNE VAASSEN

In her artistic practice, Sanne Vaassen investigates processes of change in cultural and natural phenomena by working with materials affected by the actors involved.

JONMAR VAN VLIJMEN

Jonmar van Vlijmen is an artist who researches historical, cultural, and potential transformations of ecosystems and their possibilities of evolving humans. Since 2013, Van Vlijmen has been part of the artist collective de Onkruidenier, which he co-founded.

MÜGE YILMAZ

Müge Yilmaz is a visual artist whose research presents speculations influenced by feminist science fiction and processes potential futures through installation, performance, and photography.

IMAGE CREDITS

1   Michel Faulte, Myrrha, being trans-formed into the myrrh tree, gives birth to Adonis, 1619, engraving.
2   Wilfried Walta / Anefo, Christmas tree in front of town hall Gouda (NL), 1963, photograph.
3   Central Tibetian artist, Amitabha, the Buddha of the Western Pure Land (Sukhavati), ca. 1700, painted textile. Purchase, Barbara and William Karatz Gift and funds from various donors, 2004.
4   Unknown, Beaver cutting tree, unknown, photograph.
5   Rob C. Croes, Tree affected by sour rains with crane, 1983, photograph
6   William Alfred Delamotte, Landscape with a large tree, 1802, etching.
7   Rijksvoorlichtingsdienst, Divi divi tree affected by the wind on Bonaire, unknown, photograph.
8   Mosquitos, Mosquito breeding ground in a hole in a tree trunk: museum exhibit, 1900–1930, photograph.
9   F.N. Broers, Tree crashes on car, 1963, photograph.
10 Unknown, The Tree of Life, first half of 17th century, embroidered textile.
11 Robert McCormick, Baobab tree (Adansonia digitata L.) with swollen trunk, 1884, lithograph.
12 Chancay maker in Peru, Tree, 2nd–14th century, textile sculpture. Bequest of Jane Costello Goldberg, from the Collection of Arnold I. Goldberg, 1986.
13 ANP, Collision near Hulshorst, 1954, photograph.
14 Oluf Olufsen Bagge, Yggdrasil, The Mundane Tree, 1847, colored engraving.
15 Heidemij, Big hollow tree housing a chapel, unknown, photograph.
16 John Ogilby, Ants are swarming around the base of a hollow tree while the queen ant is talking to a grass-hopper, 1666, etching.
17 Jacopo Ligozzi, The chapel of the beech tree on Mount La Verna; Christ appearing to a monk named Giovanni, 1612, engraving.
18 Claus van Amsberg, Prins Willem-Alexander in a hollow tree, 1974, photograph.
19 Thomas Daniell, Banyan tree with Hindu temples at Agori, Bihar, 1796, colored aquatint.
20 Unknown, South America; Three yellow-throated sloths clambering up a tree, unknown, colored lithograph.
21 Creijton, [...] / Anefo, Storm damage in Amsterdam, 1954, photograph.
22 Koen Suyk, Prins Bernhard plants a tree, 1977, photograph.

23 Heidemij, A pruned silver maple, unknown, photograph.
24 John Parkingson, Paradisi in sole paradisus terrestris, 1629, woodcut.
25 John Case, Illustration from Compendium anatomicum, 1696, etching.
26 W. Dickes & Co., Four twigs with catkins, all from named types of poplar or aspen (Populus species), 1855, colored Lithograph.
27 Toraja, Sulawesi, Maa cloth with Tree of Life, 19th century, Printed Textile (Vlisco) Funds from various donors, 2015.
28 A.E. Waite and Pamela C. Smith, The Suit of Wands, 1909, Tarot deck.
29 Adriaen Pietersz. van de Venne, Depiction of Human, 1656, engraving.
30 Urs Graf, Death in a Tree, 1524, engraving.
31 Follower of Luigi Garzi, Myrrha, being transformed into the myrrh tree, gives birth to Adonis, 1638–1721, oil painting.
32 Walter Crane, Genesis 3.4 , Serpens decipit Evam, 1899, photogravure.
33 Unknown, Indian woman at a tree, 1800–1899, gouache.
34 Unknown, Plan of a dummy tree observation post, 1916, UK Ministery of Information, IWM (Q 17811).
35 Rob Bogaerts, Tree fell during a storm, 1986, photograph.
36 Unknown, Artificial Christmas Tree, 1911, Patent, National Archives at College Park, NAID: 55302504.
37 Unknown, Female soldiers dance around a tree in Indonesia, 1949, photograph.
38 Heidemij, Tree ready for transportation, 1972, photograph.
39 Unknown, Cut tree is pushed aside by soldiers, 1946, photograph.
40 Nicolas Andry de Boisregard, Orthopedia, 1743, etching.
41 Rob Bogaerts, Tree in traffic, 1984, photograph.
42 W. F. de Bois Maclaren, The Rubber Tree Book, An Old Tree attacked by Boring Beetles, Maclaren & sons, 1913, p. 279.
43 Brian Grogan, Tunnel tree Toulumne Grove, 2001, Library of Congress Prints and Photographs Division Washington.

Wellcome collection
1, 6, 8, 11, 16, 17, 19, 20, 24, 25, 26, 29, 30, 31, 32, 33, 40

Nationaal Archief CC0
2, 4, 5, 7, 9, 13, 15, 21, 22, 23, 35, 37, 38, 41

Collection Metropolitan Museum of Art
3, 10, 12, 27

A Tree,
A Reader on Arboreal Kinship
Edited by Marjolein van der Loo

With written contributions by:
Joss Allen, Céline Baumann, Bárbara Sánchez Barroso,
Jorge Menna Barreto, Renée Bus, Lucy Davis, Amirio
Freeman, Manjot Kaur, Marjolein van der Loo, Karen
Lofgren, Anne Richter, Jerrold Saija, Oscar Salguero,
Jonmar van Vlijmen, Müge Yilmaz

With visual contributions by:
Gerbrand Burger, Chihiro Geuzenbroek, Femke Habets,
Roderick Hietbrink, Ingela Ihrman, Mari Keski-Korsu,
Alice Ladenburg, Hira Nabi, Frank Resseler, Sanne Vaassen

The text *The Sleep of Plants* by Anne Richter was
previously published by PMPress.org in the book Sisters
of the Revolution: A Feminist Speculative Fiction
Anthology in 2015.

Graphic design: ... Studio Yannick Nuss
Proofread by: .... Jesse Muller, Copy editing of
.... introduction by Harriet Foyster
Published by: .... Onomatopee Projects, Eindhoven,
.... Netherlands, Jesse Muller and
.... Natasha Rijkhoff
Typefaces: .... Bookman, Courier, Frankfurter,
.... Hobo, IM Fell Old English,
.... LED Dot-Matrix, New Rail Alphabet
Paper: .... Caribic (Ziegelrot) 90 g/m², 250 g/m²
Printed by: .... AS Printon
Edition: 3500
Year: .... 2026, Third Print

ISBN: 978-94-93382-07-7   **Onomatopee #258**

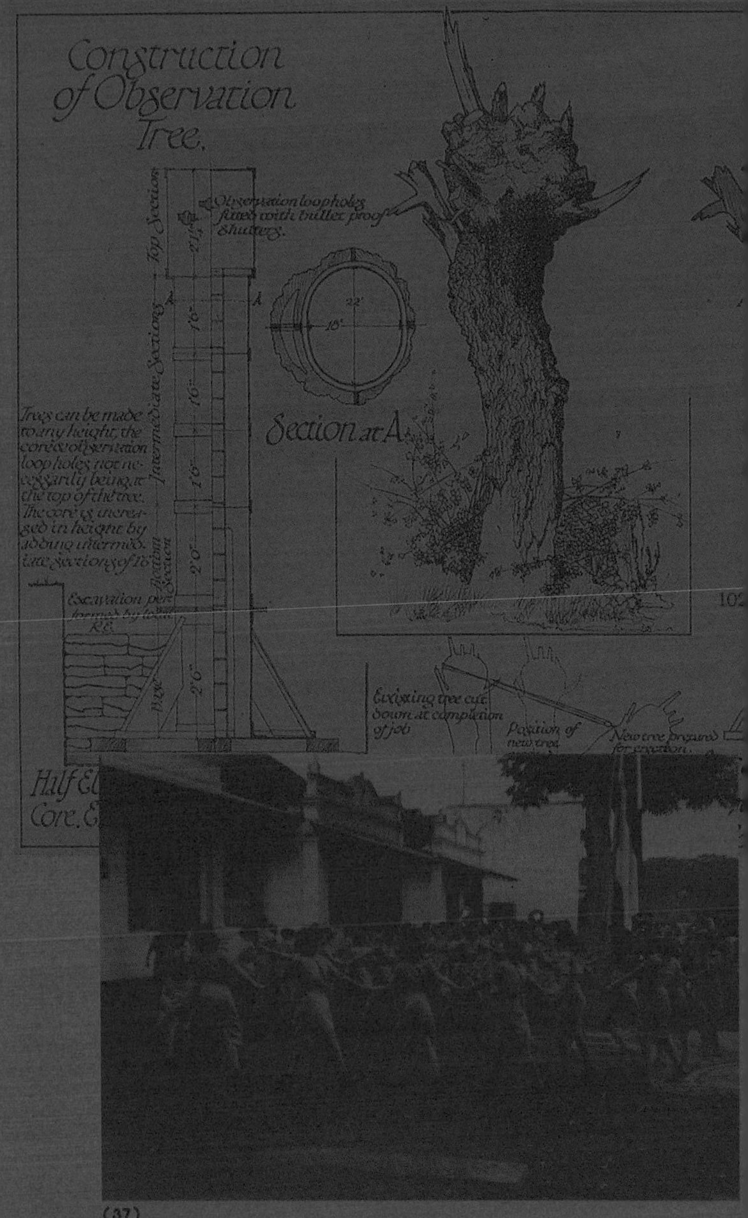

Construction of Observation Tree.
Top Section
Observation loopholes fitted with bullet proof shutters.
Intermediate Sections
Section at A
22"
18"
Trees can be made to any height, the cores & observation loop holes not necessarily being at the top of this tree. The core is increased in height by adding intermediate sections of 10...
Bottom Section
Excavation performed by team R.E.
Half El
Core. &
Existing tree cut down at completion of job
Position of new tree
New tree prepared for erection
102